deeper

First published in 2018
by Eyewear Publishing Ltd
Suite 38, 19-21 Crawford Street
London, W1H 1PJ
United Kingdom

Graphic design by Edwin Smet
Author photograph by Elizabeth Kneafsey
Printed in England by TJ International Ltd, Padstow, Cornwall

Set in Bembo 12 / 15 pt
ISBN 978-1-912477-78-4

WWW.EYEWEARPUBLISHING.COM

deeper

J M RICHARDS

EYEWEAR PUBLISHING

For Harry James

Awareness & Change

Relationships & Fruitfulness

Preface by the publisher

It is a great joy to be able to offer *deeper* as a gift to the world. I am not its author, of course, but a publisher is a midwife to the book, helping it to come into the world. We know the state the world is in – may have always been in – and so we need this book as much as at any time before in our human history.

John's book is powerful, poignant, poetic. Reading it the first time, I was deeply moved by its sincerity, and its clear reader-centred love. *Deeper*, unlike many self-help or inspirational guides, doesn't hand out easy candies for the soul. It doesn't offer gimmicks, or quick fixes. Instead, it wants you, me – every one – to shoulder the pain and mystery of existence, and by going to the core of human experience, reflect on how change happens – when it does – not to escape the challenges of life – but in transcendent acceptance of them.

John is exceptionally empathetic, and his adult life has been one of facing the gap we all have inside (his term, discussed here) between darkness and light. As a poet for over 30 years, who has worked as a poetry tutor with many new and leading poets, I can only welcome his description of the modest, yet necessary, model for self-reflection based on writing and thinking.

Many mindfulness works emphasise meditation, but John goes deeper into asking us to become active makers of our own improving conditions – he wants us to think again, and renew our world. Many gurus and philosophers, sinners and saints, have trod these paths – wisdom-writing is a genre older than any other – and John does not pretend to always be entirely original. Instead, he dispenses with any attempt at all to persuade us, or impress us, with credentials, or exceptionally complex theorising.

John's book is a wound healing as one reads it – it is raw, painful, shocking, with all the basic vivacity of any real fact of our bodily presence. I came away knowing I could use this book to go deeper within myself – a task I know that, even after a life-time of reading and study and writing, I constantly seek to evade – because, narcissism aside – truly seeing one's soulface, and accepting it, is the first – maybe the only – step to finding love for one's neighbours as well.

John's book touched me especially when he explores, in a later chapter, how lost we are all becoming in a social media saturated world of public appearances, where we lose our ability to be alone with our self, and where we lose boundaries that can keep us sane. This is a book I will go back to again and again, as I continue my own personal journey. I'm very thankful I have *deeper* with me on the adventure ahead.

Dr Todd Swift
Poet-in-residence (Visiting Scholar)
Cambridge University, Pembroke College
October 1 2017-September 30 2018

Foreword

As I thought about why I wanted to write this book it occurred to me that I have spent nearly all of my personal and professional lives pursuing close and real relationships with other people. In fact, almost everything in my life since birth has had a strong emphasis on intimacy with others and on interdependent community.

I was brought up and lived out my childhood in a community rather than in a conventional family unit, and the most significant part of my education was amongst a group comprising numerous nationalities. Since then, I have spent nearly twenty years of my life attempting to establish and nurture one living community or another and witnessing diverse people from completely different backgrounds trying to live, grow and progress together.

I have always been fascinated by intimacy and learning about other people. I have spent many thousands of hours of my life listening to and communicating with an enormous range of clients and friends about the inner workings of their lives and relationships – experiencing and watching the way that people live and think.

I have learnt so very much from those around me and changed so deeply myself.

I have known the immense privilege of being closely involved in the journey of others who have walked beside me
through the struggles and wonder of our difficult lives.

And now I realise that the main thing I have learnt in it all is
that really, I know so very little and that life and people are
more complex and mysterious than I can ever understand.
I am attempting to write about truth and to explore a little
of what I have seen and heard but every time I think about
what I really want to say, I am arrested by this realisation.

So I must be willing to simply explore, to searchingly write
about some of these things with the profound knowledge
that you and I can only approach truth, and never possess it.

If you continue to read then this book will be a journey for
us both. My own developing story has become based upon
four themes that I hope you will keep in mind as you read
the chapters that follow. I have come to believe with all of
my heart that these principles are the foundations on which
life must be built if it is to be really experienced in all of its
painful struggle and joyful beauty.

Awareness is made manifest in the recognition that we
know little and that we live in a universe of profound mystery. In our responsive willingness to continually accept
wonder and uncertainty we must become curious and ad-
venturous seekers of truth.

In the light of such patient exploration and discovery and
if we are real and sincere, we find ourselves desirous of

Change, seeking greater development within, as we become challenged and excited about the prospect of inner growth.

Furthermore, we are ever increasingly aware of and likely to invest in that which is most important; Relationships – our spiritual communion within, and then our interaction with those around us.

Finally, we realise that what brings joy and invests our lives with meaning and value is for us to become Fruitful, bearing a harvest of life in ourselves and in others through those things that we learn to invest in and to prioritise.

I hope that I will be able to enable us to simply consider and think about these four transcendent and life-giving values. They are so precious to me, and will be underpinning and informing the ideas and chapters that follow. I will return to them for the final conclusion of this book.

It is also essential that you proceed with caution and doubt and test everything I say, discarding what does not ring true.

In fact, my deepest hope for this collection of writing, is not that you will consider yourself persuaded by the thoughts that follow – but instead that in reading you may be inspired to grapple with and wonder deeply about *what it is that you think*; and that in some way such a process will prove to be an adventure and a profound blessing, just as it has been and continues to be so for me.

I wonder if at times this book may even trouble you in the reading, just as it troubled me in the writing – but I hope that above all else that if you do continue to read, that I may make you wonder and feel, and that you might freshly re-examine what you really think about that which is so rarely talked about, but that echoes somewhere deep within our subconscious.

I hope that I will help you to *think*; that you will turn these things over in your heart and your mind like my little boy examining stones on the beach opposite in the sunshine; with an open mind and simply because he is full of wonder and curiosity at what is around him. I hope that maybe you will be willing to travel with me and that we can think and learn and be curious together.

I dare to guess that only a small percentage of those who begin this book will continue, because of the considerable effort and challenge involved in thinking about the implications for life.

In our modern world we have become so used to being constantly entertained, comforted and anaesthetised, rather than challenged to think deeply and reflectively about our true selves.

Consequently, to face reality and things as they actually *are*, is the hardest thing of all for a modern human, and everything within us and in our culture mitigates against true reflection, because to pursue it is entirely dependent upon ongoing acceptance of those two great fears of humanity: uncertainty and pain.

Instead we desperately pursue significance through personal success, wealth and security, oblivious to the fact that we are choosing blindness rather than life.

Then we live out our days perpetually confused as to why we always feel the need to strive, and the presence of a gnawing emptiness. Worse, we often remain frustrated at life because our human pride has rendered us completely deceived about our place and purpose in the breathtaking wildness and beauty of this great universe.

Many millennia ago, a great and wise king exclaimed that 'there is nothing new under the sun', and I recognise that nothing of what I express will be revelatory.

Overwhelmingly, it seems to me that our problem is not that we have not heard or known the deepest truths, but that we are unable to remember; and even less to live out the practical application of their meaning by bravely taking responsibility and acting upon them.

I hope that what follows might simply be a reminder of that which you wonder about deep down, and is hopefully exciting and joyful to hear above the noise and busyness of modern life.

I have few letters after my name, and nor am I a celebrated academic or acclaimed author.

I am probably like you.

I am just someone who thinks.

I am simply someone who hopes to explore, communicate and share a glimpse of those mysterious and beautiful truths that transcend us both, but that our lives revolve around in the same way that our earth steps gracefully around the sun.

I hope that you will read what follows over many weeks, slowly and patiently; no more than one chapter at any one time, affording yourself ample time to digest, consider, re-read and weigh the ideas therein.

This book is structured in two parts, with concise chapters that have been designed to be read in this way so that they can be *reflected* upon.

The first part – containing 15 evolving themes – is intended to encourage you to explore yourself in what may be a new way, drawing you onwards as you advance toward a deeper place of discovery and awareness within.

The second part is a collection of individually themed chapters that are intended to challenge and inspire you to re-examine your own story and relationships, as you consider life freshly from a place that has always been waiting deep within your heart.

Finally, I hope that you will not undertake this expedition alone.

I encourage you to set off with someone you would like to walk with, with whom you would value growing closer, and would cherish talking more with about the *deeper* things under the surfaces of your lives, as you both navigate the great adventure of this difficult and hazardous and exhilarating path we call 'Life'.

May you embark upon a quest of greater intimacy together and agree to steadily and unhurriedly step forward; reading a chapter at a time and taking opportunity to think and to talk and to wonder about your thoughts and responses to what you have read.

As you explore, may the gentle process of reading, thinking, discussion and sharing be a precious adventure of discovery, and a true deepening of your relationship with yourself and with one another.

Introduction

We live in a fantasy world, a world of illusion.
The great task in life is to find reality.

Iris Murdoch

Awareness is the inner discovery of truth; of revealed knowledge about our hearts, our true selves, and of life itself.

It is the seeing of things, perhaps for the first time, as they really are.

Such understanding seldom falls upon us.

Instead, it must be dug patiently from the rocky terrain of life, by the few willing to look *deeper* – those willing to persistently explore the wildness and mystery within and around us.

Such exploration requires us to invest time and effort in a practice that seems increasingly rare in our modern culture of relentless 'connected' busyness: *reflection*.

Reflection is the foundation of all great human understanding; in education, writing, art, science, and invention.

Just as Albert Einstein concluded: 'I think and think for months and years. Ninety-nine times the conclusion is false. The hundredth time I am right.'

After all of his own profound writings and at the end of his life, Socrates exclaimed: 'I know you will not believe me, but the highest form of human excellence is to question oneself, and others.' He concludes; 'I cannot teach anybody anything. *I can only make them think.*'

Reflection remains the catalyst for each and every precious human creation, achievement, revelation and discovery.

It is the root of all understanding, awareness and truth.

But in our modern world of instant information and gratification, we prioritise it little.

We are too busy, or we are on our phones.

There is always something else to watch or to do.

Thoughtful reflection is difficult, and it is time consuming.

Consequently, awareness is a journey that we can only ever embark upon if we do not count the cost, or if we can correctly perceive the alternative – which is oblivious stagnation – to be infinitely more costly to our wellbeing.

We tend instead to frantically pursue popularity, security, and success to its exclusion.

And despite the truth that awareness may well lead us to achieve these ends, it is almost always only achieved through their initial sacrifice.

This sacrifice requires great bravery. In the words of Marianne Williamson: 'It takes courage to endure the sharp pains of self-discovery, rather than choose to take the dull pain of unconsciousness that would last the rest of our lives.'

Such painful discovery requires us to navigate the exploration of our true nature as a spiritual being; and learn to accept both sides of our heart; our darkness and our beauty, our brokenness and our strength.

If only we are willing, this acceptance gently leads us into a place of quiet inner surrender where we no longer feel the perpetual need to strive.

It is from this quiet place that we finally begin to see and to experience life in all of its true beauty and glorious potential.

Such surrender might be better described as our ultimate acceptance of humility.

In practice, it represents the end of our own certainty, our desire for control – the giving up of our relentless selfish will. Inner submission finally opens our eyes to the truth and mystery that lie beyond us; beckoning us into wholeness and life.

Such a remarkable opening might be better described in the words of the Japanese Zen Masters who say: 'Do not seek the truth. Just drop your opinions.'

We must think upon these ancient words: 'Whoever seeks to preserve his life will lose it, but whoever loses his life, will keep it.'

Only through this 'losing' can our human eyes ever be opened.

I am overwhelmed by the realisation that this is such a hard thing to explore and to communicate, from one to another, in writing or in speech.

I can only hope that over the course of these following chapters I am somehow helped by an invisible Grace in which I trust, and enabled by that great Force around and within us that leads us to all truth, if only we search in hopeful sincerity.

As we begin our journey, I must lay a crucial cornerstone that I believe with all of my heart:

There is only one foundation to true awareness and although it may seem very simple; it appears to me to actually be extremely rare.

It is terribly, terribly important, and it is this:

In truth, all of us have an incomplete view and we must accept this daily and walk humbly.

We are all searchers, explorers, pilgrims and though we may feel that we have accumulated more 'truth' than others, we must constantly remind ourselves that our own precious pieces, however consuming and non-negotiable to us, *are part of a puzzle that is so large, so magnificent and so complex that we are only ever glimpsing a small section of something that utterly dwarfs and transcends us.*

There is nothing more corrupting and dangerous than giving in to the deeply human temptation to simplify and shortcut the journey; the futile sickness of believing we are the sole owners and bearers of the 'truth' and that we have all the answers.

The darkest of our beautiful mankind's manifold curses is that thanks to religion, ideology and individualism, humanity is tragically stacked full of those who genuinely think like this: that their view is the *right* way and that anyone outside of their narrow frame of reference is wrong and misguided.

Such mindsets have underpinned and caused the great majority of suffering throughout human history and continue to wreak havoc with our vulnerable and infant humanity wherever they may be found.

True awareness is the exact opposite and it is a remarkable and wonderful paradox in that the more that grace allows us to see, the more our sight reveals how very little we really know and if only we will quietly follow we are led into a calm and gentle humility.

This humility is our greatest friend.

If we abandon it, whether we know it or not we are utterly lost and all that lies before us is meaningless and futile.

But if we hold onto it in all things and at all costs something remarkable and transcendent occurs in the cosmos: we are somehow protected, covered and borne through the struggles of our uncertain lives along a gentle path of Grace.

This is a profound mystery and one that I am simply unable to understand, illuminate or explain. But it is a mystery that that only humility can bring.

I hope that as we step forward together we will hear the music of its quiet beauty, and find shelter beneath its cool shade.

Awareness
& Change

Integrity & Paradox

The path to Holiness lies in questioning everything.
Seek and ye shall find enough pieces of truth to be able to start
fitting them together.
You will never be able to complete the puzzle.
But you will be able to fit together enough pieces to begin to
get glimpses of the big picture and to see
that it is very beautiful indeed.
M Scott Peck

If I am going to try to approach truth in human life and relationships, I must begin by thinking about Integrity and Paradox.

These two principles underpin all truth and I must constantly remind myself of their importance in order to balance my quest for reality.

Integrity

Integrity is often thought of as the same thing as transparency and honesty. But integrity is best described as so much more than this: it is the ability and more importantly the will to view things with a complex approach that 'integrates' more than one or two or even three or more diverse viewpoints.

It is the awareness to weigh and assess and think about things in a multi-faceted and complex way and to thoroughly reject one dimensional, judgmental, simplistic and clumsy thinking.

It is the gift of thinking with wisdom.

Those who think with integrity tend to learn its ways patiently and accumulate it increasingly as they progress through life and it is revealed to them that people and things are overwhelmingly complex, and can only be accurately viewed as such. It is a skill that the wise recognise must be central to any sense of knowledge and experience that they may possess.

Thinkers driven by integrity are patient, curious, open, and above all of those things, humble. They recognise that their view and vision of things may well be and invariably is incomplete – but importantly, they are simultaneously brave enough to make the best decision they can when necessary, even when they recognise that their information may be limited.

Those who possess and practice integrity are the bravest and the wisest amongst us.

If there was one thing that I could wish for myself to have considered earlier in what remains the relentless work to overcome my lifelong tendency toward dogma and proud ignorance, it would be to have understood life and truth to be best viewed in this complex, patient and curious way.

Paradox

And so I progress to paradox, another fundamental foundation in my search for truth. One good way to try to consider paradox is that it is really at its most basic level about acceptance – about our willingness as thinkers and explorers to accept the truthfulness of two seemingly opposing realities and to be willing to take the time and effort that it takes to navigate between them to find the path of integrity in our journey.

When we forget and discount paradox, it is almost inevitable that we will get lost; for to abandon it is to be simplistic and naive and discounts the effort of the real work of pursuing truth. Though this is an attractive and easy option and one I have chosen more times than I can remember, it never leads to real understanding or lasting change.

Instead, we must be willing to be brave and to abandon our simplistic thinking and to understand that for almost every truth that we find, there is an opposing reality that will almost certainly be true, and somewhere between the two; in the tension, there will be the narrow way that leads to life – but it may take persistent negotiation and flexibility with much effort and work to find.

From the great truths at the heart of ancient spiritual revelation to the simple ones inherent to the mechanics of family life, nearly all true reality and wisdom is essentially paradoxical.

Fascinatingly, it is when humankind takes only one side of a paradox, and follows it as the only truth, that certain danger lies.

Communism and Capitalism are good examples of this: Take either as an absolute truth and principle to live by as large parts of the world have done for much of the last century, and the result will be utterly disastrous for many. But take them as opposing elements of and differing parts of a complex solution; and they can be useful and full of value to society.

As history reveals, the all-encompassing doctrines of organised Religion are at risk of being their most toxic to individuals and communities when as appears so tragically common around the world, just one side of their complex ancient theologies are trumpeted to the detriment of their balancing alternatives; resulting in an incoherent and destructive message of ideological pride and imbalance.

In contrast, in the places where conscientious balance and the corresponding love and calm tolerance are fought for and championed, the outcome is inevitably one of peace and hope to fragile communities in need of forgiveness and grace. Post-apartheid South Africa would be one good example of just such a wisely led dynamic bringing great hope and healing out of a deep societal wound following years of violence and mistrust.

On a more individual level, one example of fundamental paradoxical truth is found in the phenomenon of control:

In one sense it is crucial that we are carefully controlling of our feelings, lives and emotions as much as we possibly can be and it is only by this control that we begin to be free.

But it is also simultaneously true that true freedom in ourselves is found in our surrender; our willingness to completely let go, and to accept that we are powerless and our control must be completely given up.

As a final illustration, I think about the example of living paradox that can be found in our relationships around honesty.

Consider that, it is essential that we have honesty within our intimate relationships such as marriage. But within honesty and within marriage, one must learn to show discretion in the name of wisdom and love rather than to tell one's loved one everything. And of course, one of the chief skills that we must learn and negotiate around healthy honesty in our intimate relationships is when *is the right time to pour out, and when it is wiser and more loving to withhold*.

Herein is real wisdom, herein is real Love.

In conclusion, Integrity and Paradox must be our great friends and our trustworthy guides as we learn to navigate the great expanses of life, seeking answers and truth. They must be at the very heart of our thoughts and we must beware of their absence in anything that we think and embark upon.

We must navigate only within their shadow – like the sun by day and the moon by night – as we cast off from the shore of our safe and one-dimensional thinking, and allow ourselves to drift out across the water into the mysterious blue ebb of a gentle and unknown tide.

Of All Deceivers Fear Most Thyself.

Søren Kierkegaard

In order to become increasingly aware, one of the primary things that we must be willing to do is to explore our true selves; *us as we really are.*

Though this is such an exciting journey and the most powerful that we can ever embark upon, it is simultaneously traumatic and must be prioritised in the face of the constant temptation to stop altogether.

As we discover truths that are unpalatable about ourselves, we face an enormous battle if we are not to pander to our overwhelming ego seeking to constantly drag us from reality and back into the comfort of our complacent individualism.

Our entire modern culture is structured to distract us from looking at who we really are and the difficult work of our inner journey, because such work requires the two things that we prioritise least: *time and reflection.*

Furthermore, humans who are self-aware and understand who they really are, will not buy and desire *things* relentlessly, or give their time solely to the pursuit of success.

Consequently, this revelation is simply incompatible with what our society requires of us to maintain its ravenous appetite for our constant spending.

Capitalism requires the sacrifice of our souls for its relentless drive towards 'growth' and we offer them gladly.

We frantically pursue security and wealth, and yet the self-attention and nurture that we need most evade us. Modern life simply steals them from us, and we are not self-aware enough to miss them or to get them back.

A good way for us to understand and measure this phenomenon is to ask ourselves when we last had an hour alone, undistracted and quiet, in which we had the opportunity and peace to think about ourself and how we are doing.

In fact, we become addicted to filling our free time with more 'things' and spend longer at work or on our phones, feeling that we are 'connected' when the most crucial person to connect to and invest in, ourselves, is left alone and slowly withers away.

This is why children are infinitely more alive and well than us – more capable of happiness and joy than adults; because their inner life and self-communion has not yet had time to be extinguished.

As they grow older and the overwhelming emptiness of adulthood in a materialist culture is forced upon them, they develop the emptiness that we know only too well. We call it 'growing up' and are relieved that they stop asking awkward questions when in fact they are growing numb and blind like us.

Actually, the greatest and most valuable of all gifts we could possibly give to our children is to *daily exemplify a person who honestly knows themselves and in that knowledge is able to consistently demonstrate self-love, self-accountability and self-nurture.*

When I work with parents around this phenomenon and think about myself as a father, I witness the most profound truth: We are aware enough to know that this is the most important thing of all but we are rendered helpless to teach it despite our desire and longing to do so.

Instead, we know that we are unable to teach it because we don't practise it.

We do not have it within ourselves and it can only be instilled by example.

So it is better to suppress what we really know, and in order to quieten our guilt, we give our children far too many things and thus distract them.

Ultimately, when we have made them suppressing and forgetful of truth just like us, we are surprised and confused when they develop our same problems, our familiar issues.

Indeed, the internet, television and the relentless demands of our busy lives mean that we are constantly bombarded by information, products and images that monopolise our attention.

Individualism and materialism only need appeal to our hunger: our ravenous desire to feel better about ourselves driven by the subconscious knowledge of our true fragility. Then, we will barely think about anything at all. In fact, we tend only to give attention to what makes us feel good and what we have to do next.

This is our humanity.

Consequently, the journey of inner discovery is at best sporadic and is nearly always only considered in the most extreme conditions of personal duress, precipitated through conditions such as personal crisis of some kind: the breakdown of a relationship, illness, bereavement, alcoholism, depression or psychological breakdown. This is because these occurrences tend to simply expose our true vulnerability and us as we really are and force us to address the reality of our human fragility and brokenness.

This brokenness is invariably avoided or rationalised by humans at all costs who fear and mistrust it above all else.

But in fact, it is a great and wonderful gift for those that have walked its graceful path.

While many may perceive that the individuals who have not been exposed to such obvious breaking as being the strong healthy ones, in fact, it is often those who have not been in touch with and faced their own brokenness that are found to be the most lost; labouring under a deception that works only in context of their own oblivion to reality. Conversely, true awareness despite its certain pain and inherent suffering is a wonderful journey containing endless reward, if only we can continue in our bravery and willingness to negotiate that which is yet to be discovered within.

On our journey, primarily we must first face a crucial and foundational truth about our humanity which few will ever approach or understand because it is at odds with the way that we like to live in comfort and complacency:

It is the truth that we are at our core a paradoxical being.

We contain both the propensity for tremendous good, and for great evil.

In our deepest parts, we are simultaneously both light and dark, truthful and self-deceiving, glorious and yet vulnerable.

And perhaps the fundamental wound that has harmed humanity most, is our profound human resistance to such awareness — because we like to think instead that we are fundamentally good and that everything is fine, and we desire above all else, comfort and ease.

Easily, we suppress any knowledge of our true darkness — in fact the most damaged among us do all that is within their power to bury and obscure any revelation of their own fallibility and lostness.

And it is this suppression and self-deception that is at the root of all human evil.

Notice that I don't suggest that our wicked behaviours or actions are the root of our evil but instead, our refusal to bravely acknowledge, meet and expose our orientation to that evil that is at the root of our peculiar lostness.

And the simple reason for this is that the evil that exists in part of who we are is *real; and the* consequences of its outworking, if unchecked, may be catastrophic — as one cannot avoid in reading the daily news or a cursory study of mankind's history.

The more that we run from facing such evil and pretend that it does not live in us, the more we give it overwhelming power.

The more we try to push it into the darkness, the more we render ourselves powerless to resist it, master it and practise love in its place.

Yet the defeat of individual human evil is only possible through our humble willingness to confess firstly to ourselves and then to those around us that we contain not only light, but also darkness within.

We are paradoxical beings, and must consistently and achingly drag the shadows of our darkness into the light through honesty and humility in discipline that is sustained and lifelong.

And this is why true awareness and spiritual wholeness is so staggeringly rare in humans.

Because it is bloody, painful and difficult.

In my behaviours and outlook I find that daily it is overwhelmingly easier to hide such revelation, and to pretend that I am OK and good and nothing need be examined or discovered within and such possibilities should be left alone.

But the very real and catastrophic problem with this simplistic conclusion, is that it is only a half truth, one side of an essentially understood paradox.

We are lovely; in fact, we can be more supremely beautiful than most of us have ever dared believe even in our wildest imaginings.

But the key to the unlocking of this beauty is actually found only in first exposing and then facing the very real darkness that lives in part of our souls.

This knowledge cannot really be taught. It can only be discovered; accepted within – and then lived out.

This is Awareness.

To summarise: much of our deeply human psychological darkness and individual spiritual malaise is caused by our profound unwillingness to bring our true predicament into the light of truth and make an ongoing decision to confront and do battle with our dark side. Instead, many of us are willingly consigned to an existence of simplistic delusion, believing that people are either good and right, or bad and wrong and inevitably deciding that they are in the former camp and that there is nothing more to be considered.

The truth is that all of us *are simultaneously both*.

Furthermore, while there are certainly some largely evil people in the world and others who are tremendously good, one of the things that makes those most healthy and well among us so, is their constant and ongoing insistence on their own brokenness and willingness to continually wrestle with their weaknesses.

It is in this cumulative and lifelong humility that such people find their limitless ability to be fruitful and to do real good.

Isn't this a wonderful paradox!

The Most Important Relationship of All

The greatest thing in the world is to know how to belong to oneself.

Michel de Montaigne

We cannot even begin to attempt to explore awareness without discussing the most important of all the relationships that we in our paradoxical humanity can ever pursue: our relationship with ourselves.

Though this may be an idea that many have never considered and much less prioritised, the truth is that at the very centre of our own individual story, each and every one of us *has an ongoing relationship with ourselves*. This relationship begins from the moment we become conscious that we are a separate being from our parents and from others, usually thought to be at around 6-months old and can think *of* ourselves and *for* ourselves.

From this point forward and to a lesser or greater extent depending on our unique psyche, we will grow and develop a view of ourself as an individual and more importantly a way of relating to ourself – a self-awareness. It is within this self-regard and self-communication that power in our lives and destinies lies. No other relationship can or will control our direction, our fate and our future to the extent that the choices and path we pursue in this intimate dialogue and story do so.

The only path to wellbeing and peace is to courageously develop a truthful and healthy relationship with ourselves.

There is no shortcut, no substitute, no alternative.

There is no healing for our wounds nor any change and progress available to humanity outside of the acceptance of responsibility for and the healthy pursuit of this relationship. Despite the thousands of deceptive alternatives that we ourselves, our fellow humans and our culture regularly offer us, there is no way to circumvent this crucial truth; that we must learn to become aware of, relate to and govern ourselves in truth and love, in accountability and grace, in self-discipline and self-encouragement.

It is only in accepting this foundational truth and then daily taking its considerable responsibility upon ourselves and prioritising this relationship above all else that we may find the path that leads to healing and life.

A simple metaphor to describe these things might be to imagine our psyche and wellbeing as our own garden. Just like a garden, our minds and spirits contain their own limited landscape and yet exist in the context of external weather over which we often have minimal or no control – our lives are invariably just the same, subject to external childhoods, backgrounds, experiences, people and problems that we must respond to.

Just like a garden, if we are to flourish, we as people require thoughtful and ongoing nurture in the way that we facilitate growth, eradicate unwanted incursions and respond daily to outside factors. In accepting the immense import of our relationship with ourself, we are recognising that not only is our internal garden vulnerable and dependent on such nurture, but that we ourselves must become the diligent gardener of our own souls: watering, pruning and planting.

Only to the extent that we can become a fully responsible, committed and wise gardener will we ever see lasting healing and spiritual growth and find the way that leads to life. To become such a gardener is the most important pursuit of our lives but it is also the most difficult. It is a long, sometimes lonely and often laborious road.

To remain on it requires an immense amount of time, commitment, tenacity and resilience.

We cannot find nor survive this road without outside help but we must often walk alone.

At times it is completely dark and we must simply press on in hope and in faith.

But we must walk, on and on and on; stumbling, striving, dancing...

with an unshakeable resolve that must never die.

Awareness of Love

We have all heard it said: 'Love thy neighbour as thyself.'

This is considered amongst the greatest of all truths. As a statement it is deeply powerful and yet disarmingly simple.

For centuries people have been guided and inspired by the truth contained therein.

But beneath the obvious meaning – that we must treat others as we ourselves would like to be treated – there is something much deeper conveyed, and something that is intensely important.

We can only love others to the extent that we do love and have loved ourselves.

The simple reality is: that we are only able to give to those around us that which we have accepted, worked through and appropriated within.

We cannot truly love another, unless we have first loved ourselves and more importantly embarked upon our inner work of love.

One of the most damaging confusions produced by our fragmented and pressurised culture, is that so very commonly a person will join him or herself to another in order to avoid and flee this work.

More perplexingly, many individuals will invariably take this step in the name of 'love'. Such people naturally think of themselves as 'lovers' but in fact, they are emotionally parasitic – their own identity and wellbeing is solely driven and sustained through their connection to another person or thing – invariably someone or something that they feel genuinely that they 'love' passionately.

And the reason for this needy attachment is that at root, such people do not know themselves to be independently loved and accepted in themselves and by themselves. They are often wounded and lost people. Unsurprisingly, they turn out to be needy, demanding and controlling relationally and more than anything, emotionally childlike.

But more seriously, in their pursuit of and attachment to another individual to escape their own emotional lostness, such a person is unknowingly consigning themselves to a lifetime of difficult relationships, rather than the possibility of facing their true need and beginning the rocky path to healing and hope.

Furthermore, when such people carry their wounds into their 'love' relationships and when the inevitable consequences occur and cracks appear in the relationship, the irony is that they will often complain that they feel 'unloved' and feel disappointment and anger towards their partner, leading to misplaced upset and emotional trauma for both parties involved.

They live with a leaking well in their soul that can never be filled by another, no matter how much love is offered.

Only through their own courage and willingness may they begin the difficult path to wholeness by turning away from the idolisation of another person and facing that which is so painful to confront within.

In our modern world, of all the notions and ideas that mankind chases in pursuit of meaning and happiness, love is by far the most tarnished and perverted.

It is a word we hear endlessly; in music, the media, religion and in relationships – as a concept it has become overwhelmingly cheap because it is a drug so deeply desired to feed our relentless human hunger and our longing to be connected.

And although in its true nature love certainly is the most important thing of all, it is the rarest thing to find in a state of wholeness and reality amongst humans.

If we are brave, we must admit that many of us claim to love our partners, our children, our families, even our pets, on the basis of our transient feelings, without having true understanding or comprehension of what real love is, or what it actually means in practice.

Surely, there is a very good reason for this: real love is not a feeling, and it is not selfish; in fact it is not about us at all.

Real love only exists in the context of willingness, giving and in awareness.

The other things that we call love are simply comforts for us in our deep human lostness; to make us feel mistakenly self-assured that our behaviours and feelings are justified because we act out of what we mistakenly call 'love'.

In fact, any therapist or psychiatrist will tell you that 'love' is used as an excuse for the most blatant acts of human selfishness and abuse on a daily basis in a million different relationships and scenarios, whether it is through parasitic co-dependence, a controlling marriage, a bullying parent or a 'concerned' peer – the list is endless.

Humans like so much to talk and think about what they call 'love', when what they actually mean is 'want' and 'need'.

In my humanity, I talk about my 'love' for another when what I mean is 'me and my feelings'.

Some of the reasons for this are because humans are in their core nature covetous beyond all else, as evidenced so alarmingly in individualistic and capitalist cultures like my own.

In our regular state of disconnectedness and desire, we experience a gnawing hunger and loneliness within, that for a time can be filled by other people or possessions; a spouse, partner, a child, a pet, a hobby or a car.

This phenomenon feels more than acceptable if we can call what we feel for a particular entity: 'love'.

But the truth is simple and it is this: *the only extent to which we can honestly measure how much we love another person is the extent to which our existence in their life is a blessing to them, is fruitful for them.*

If our existence does not contribute to their true wellbeing and wholeness, our presence is not a loving one. Unpalatable though this simple truth is, it is sad to say that there isn't anything else.

Everything else is simply our profoundly human co-dependent desire. Though it feels comforting and helps us to avoid facing our own need, we must be brave and learn to utterly forsake it if we are to begin to truly love others.

It is easy to show 'love' on the terms and ways that we choose, in context of what we want and in the way that we want to feel that we are giving it.

But the most terrifying, dangerous and yet overwhelmingly powerful of all the things that we can say to our partner or child or friend is not 'I love you' but instead: 'What is it that I can do that makes you feel loved by me?'

In relationships where this is possible and prioritised, love and growth flows free and there is healing and hope for the struggles, hurts and challenges of modern relationships.

If we are committed to keeping life and hope alive and avoiding the astoundingly common descent into relational stagnation that blights our modern culture, we must be brave enough to ask this question regularly, gently, peacefully and with the absolute commitment not to make it all about us if the answer is not what we want to hear.

Nothing else is love.

The path of awareness is exciting and it is near, but it may be uncomfortable, difficult to negotiate and deeply challenging.

But if only we are humble and willing, we can utterly forsake the ongoing tendencies of our human selfishness and take responsibility for our own problems and feelings once and for all.

Only then may we wholeheartedly begin the work of learning to know and then love ourselves.

It is on this lifelong journey and in its practice that true love is finally born and grows.

If only we are willing, persistent love will begin to flow into our own hearts and then spread outward over those we want to love truly.

It is a wonderful love that starts as a trickle and as we continue in it and submit to its ways, turns into a great river.

Love and Change

Man cannot remake himself without suffering.
For he is both the marble and the sculptor.

Alexis Carrel

I have suggested that real love for others can only be a function of our own love for ourselves and the work and fruit of this love. But what do I mean by this? What *is* this work of love?

What does loving oneself really look like, feel like and how can it be explored and pursued?

I want to now do my best to illuminate and explore some of the principles inherent to this process and also to consider some of the things that it is not.

At the root of true love, there is a profound and beautiful paradox.

It is the paradox of *acceptance* and *change*. True love contains these two principles in a constantly evolving balance and both are essential if love for ourselves is to emerge and take root.

As we pursue awareness and begin to explore truthfully our own behaviours and psyches and if this process is real and steeped in integrity, it will certainly at times be a traumatic journey. On the way we must increasingly learn to simply *accept* ourselves as we truly are, with all of our loveliness and all of our wounds, and with no attempt to cover our own vulnerability or to justify our darkness.

We must find and develop the rare courage and true love to convince ourselves that even if we discover the most unpalatable truths about our true self, that such discovery is graciously accepted and both the realisation and the inevitable cost, is met with serenity.

But furthermore, it is important to say that self-love is not just about us being *resigned* to such discovered truths. True acceptance, love and care for ourselves is so much more than that. Self-love is not only us being brave enough and truthful enough to continually and painfully pursue the work of discovering ourselves and graciously finding things that displease us.

Most crucially of all, in allowing our wounds to be made manifest in gracious acceptance, once exposed, it is the relentless pursuit of our hard-fought victory over them, our refusal to be consigned to their power, or to continue to be identified with them in our lives and futures.

However long and whatever the cost, we must be tirelessly committed to the necessary faith, belief and most crucially the action necessary for our inner change and healing.

It is only this wonderful and blessed combination of determinations in humans that comprise true and thriving self-love that will bear a harvest of lifelong fruit in our souls.

It is only this heartfelt orientation that will fix and then maintain our course to be steered towards increasing freedom and lasting peace.

This all sounds so very intense, effortful and such a great challenge.

And at times, it is.

But what is so wonderful to be able to also convey, is this wonderful truth: when we humbly submit ourselves to these principles and willingly begin to be brave in facing and pursuing truth and then believing in and relentlessly persisting for change, something wonderful and miraculous happens: We realise that change is not only utterly and completely possible... *but that it is near.*

Change really is available and waiting quietly for us all.

Change is not elusive or impossible.

It is only *us* who live in avoidance, procrastination, and fear.

It is *we* who are cowardly and aloof.

It is only ever *ourselves* who avoid submission to and pursuit of such life-giving principles, only *we* who flee from the endless wonder and infinite possibilities of genuine progress in our hearts and lives because they require courage and persistence and faith.

If, and ultimately when, we do finally submit to this revelation and once and for all die to the immature fantasies of ego, courageously facing and embracing who we really are under it all, the powerful spell of stagnant individualism in whatever form it has been made manifest, is broken.

Suddenly we stand on the brink of an enormous power in which the possibilities for our souls and lives become limitless. Horizons are stretched beyond what we could possibly imagine and we are giddy with the joy and excitement.

Such joy is only experienced by those who know what it is to be broken, and that only in this breaking can all things become possible to them and for them.

And because such revelation requires breaking, we will only learn to pursue and to really covet it, when our eyes are opened and we realise that without it, our souls will always remain withered and we will never escape the strange kind of emptiness that we seek to quiet with our relentless pursuit of image, security, material things, relationships or success.

This is the wonderful place in which *humility and repentance bear fruit* and that true awareness has its birth.

It is here that is the quiet place of our soul's beginning, as we begin our negotiation of the narrow way that leads to life.

The path is steep and perilous.

But it is paved with life giving power, and once willingly embarked upon, we soon find that we are gently propelled by that great life force within and around us that whispers love and mercy.

For the first time, we finally begin to find joy, peace and quiet rest for ourselves on the road.

Growing Up

For narrow is the way that leads to life, and few find it.

Matthew 7, vs 14

Reading back, I realise that the principles I have been describing thus far are simply about us as unique individuals finding a congruent and genuine process of 'growing up'. Although we all age physically, it is actually a tiny percentage of us who ever reach spiritual maturity because as I have explained, the process and cost is simply consistently difficult. Furthermore, true growth happens to be entirely and solely dependent upon our willing acceptance to navigate those two great ancient fears and mistakenly perceived enemies of all mankind: mystery and pain.

Instead, the comfortable fantasies of childhood normally prevail and we invariably live out our days as ageing emotional children wrapped in the secure cocoon we have woven via the goals taught to us in genuinely good faith.

We easily settle upon a religious or societal belief system, family, house, material wealth, a career and comfortable lifestyle – in order to fend off any disturbing reminder that there might be infinitely more to this glorious and mysterious world than that which is seen before us and experienced in our feelings and through the pursuit of success, security and the achievement of our desires.

We live in a profoundly shallow and corrupt age in which religion, politics, contemporary culture and even our well-meaning parents and childhood teachers so often function within a dizzying array of assumed and unchallenged perspectives.

Such views are thrust upon us from our earliest age and perpetuated deafeningly as a result of the ravenous insecurity and need for material comfort and simplistic answers that exists in a human race increasingly aware of its overwhelming fragility in this great wild universe.

In this context, precious few people seem to learn or develop either the inclination or the necessary energy to consistently step quietly out of the things that they have been conditioned to believe and more importantly the way that they have been programmed to *feel* about life and themselves.

In a sense, we are all to a large extent, products of our parenting, culture and background, conditioned by and for a naive 'certainty' in how we are endlessly told that things simply *are*. But some of us simply need awakening and encouragement to find ourselves increasingly drawn to the great unfathomable *mystery* our subconscious recognises that we are joined to in this great Universe.

Even in the midst of our vacuous modern culture, still some of us seem to deeply feel and comprehend within, the great breath-taking *adventure* of life; to connect with the glorious joy and accept the humbling anguish of loss and pain – but most of all; to yearn for and accept questions and humility, rather than echo the glib answers with which modernity bombards our every waking moment.

Let us long for the silences and spaces and the wildness available to us, rather than the constant noise, entertainment and material shallowness of modern culture.

Let us not miss this great opportunity of our few years here: for wonder, the adventure of seeking and the joy of perpetual fresh discovery.

I see it so vividly, pure as crystal in my little boy as he grows and explores.

I long that it might remain in his fascinated unspoilt soul, untarnished and unhindered by the overwhelming dogma and emptiness of adulthood soon to be forced upon him.

Incompletion, Humility and Faith

True wisdom comes to each of us when we realise how little we understand about life, ourselves, and the world around us.

Socrates

One of the most wonderful authors I have ever read is the celebrated American Psychiatrist M. Scott Peck who became one of my favourite writers and a major influence in my teens. In his writing he describes how disappointed he was when at medical school as a young and idealist thinker in the 70s he had bitterly come to the conclusion that there were no frontiers left in science and that he would never make a great discovery as everything was already known!

Amusingly ludicrous as this now seems, he describes how the entire course and perspective of his life dramatically changed when one day he decided he would stop thinking about what was *known* scientifically, and started asking himself and his tutors what was *not known* in science about life, the natural and spiritual world and the universe. . and of course, he then realised very quickly that despite the smug scientific knowledge of his day being taught at Harvard and Oxford, that in reality we still know very little about anything!

In the words of Thomas Edison whom he quotes: *'We don't even begin to understand one percent about ninety-nine percent of anything.'* Peck goes on to discuss the gaping void between the great deal that we as postmodern humans *think* we know and feel so wise and secure in – and the staggering amount that we don't know about ourselves and our Ancient Universe.

I read recently that if our own galaxy were the size of a frozen pea and were placed on the main stage in the Albert Hall, then in comparison size-wise, even the *known* galaxies that we have been able to map would not all be able to be squeezed into the building. Indeed, as our scientific knowledge expands, more than anything else we are increasingly faced with how little we yet know and can comprehend of the great breadth of this wild and profoundly beautiful cosmos that so dwarfs us.

Closer to home, if only we are willing to think for a moment, it is remarkable just how much we *don't know* about our lives and our destiny and future.

Despite the fanatical protestations of on one side atheistic zealots and on the other religious fundamentalists, in truth the genuine cumulative learnings of gradual science reveal that despite what we may have claimed triumphantly, we really don't quite know how the universe came into being and when.

We can only be truthfully agnostic about the great questions; or hypothesise and guess – *or employ faith.*

On a more personal level, we know that we will die, but when?

We may have an intense and sincere faith, but we don't *know* what happens at the moment of death and if our spirit lives on, despite the most fanatical berating us with horror stories of nothingness or eternal torture by a 'loving' God unless we wholly agree with them and their certain conclusions on these big issues.

In answer to so many of the most fundamental questions for our human race and for our loved ones – we must answer quietly that we simply don't know.

What will become of our perishing tiny planet in this great universe? It seems increasingly possible that as a race our days are numbered... but when might they run out?

Is there life elsewhere in the vast expanse of space?

Will our children or our parents outlive us? How and when will our lives end? How many days and hours do we have? Will we leave a positive legacy?

We simply don't know.

Will our marriages last to our beloved? We must profess *hope* but in a time when nearly half of all marriages end in divorce, we can claim only that.

Will Spurs ever win the Premiership? My little boy and I dearly hope so every season and feel we must employ real *faith,* but...

I could go on, but I trust that my point is overwhelmingly clear:

To a great deal of the most important and significant questions that affect our fate most, we are clueless and despite our unending human complacency, we are little closer to finding satisfactory answers than we were at the dawn of science.

And that's really OK.

We don't need to be afraid of or to fight this realisation.

Instead, we can rather marvel at the great wonder of the mysterious and stunningly beautiful world we find ourselves so privileged to be born into, and be thankful for the little time offered to us, in which we are invited to contribute our own thread in the rich tapestry of our planet's vibrant history.

Sadly, it seems unfortunate that for so many, this place of humble wonder is a deeply unsettling and unpalatable realisation and so before even considering it and undertaking the inevitable humility and effort that its acceptance involves, we appear compelled to respond in a number of ways: Many scientific minds shelter themselves under the recent advances of modern hypotheses and congratulate themselves inwardly with all that we have been able to discover and focus on what *is* known.

Many religious people cling to dogmatic polemics, often literalising their scriptures aggressively despite the profound and sacred metaphorical contextualisation.

Such people tend to perceive any challenge to the authority of their own interpretations of ancient writings – which inevitably they are certain are 'God's intended interpretation' – as the work of the Devil.

Many others in our age simply innoculate themselves to the knowledge of their relative tiny-ness in the universe and their own human fragility and precariousness, by the materialistic accumulation of popularity, success, and financial security.

Some turn to drink, drugs, sex and the hedonistic pursuit of pleasure with the 'eat, drink and be merry for tomorrow we die' rationale.

And furthermore, many very highly intelligent and aware people of all ages that I have worked with, simply look away from such issues and reason that they will 'cross that bridge when they come to it'.

Tragically, a larger amount than I would ever have thought possible have been forced to face the reality of their own death much sooner than they expected.

You see, we just don't know.

Regardless of our response to and chosen position on the immense mystery of the Universe and our unknown longevity, place and existence therein, I wonder if there is a simple awareness and a way of looking at things that might comprise integrity and that we are all be able to subscribe to in good faith, regardless of our pre-conceived views and inevitable position.

It is the humble and curious recognition of our own ideological incompletion in the light of the enormity of the questions and mysteries facing us.

What I mean to suggest, is that if we hold a position of entirely *certain* belief – whether it is in atheism, secular humanism, Islam, Buddhism, or Christianity – we should be fully respected, listened to and honoured in our community and society and allowed to practise and live out our beliefs (providing of course that they don't impinge upon others' wellbeing).

But I wonder if more of us need to be brave enough and employ the *integrity* necessary, to acknowledge that our individual position is just that – one of our personal conviction and *faith* rather than one of fanatical *certainty* for which there is no need.

Surely, each of us should be able to take a great pride in the sincerity of their personal belief and be honoured for it, but the world would certainly be a more healthy and safe place if those zealous ones amongst us would accept and even embrace the fact that in a great deal of cases and on a great deal of issues, their position is simply *one that they must employ faith to sustain*, and not the established fact that they are so certain of.

Moreover this orientation is just how it *should* be and is actually in keeping with a wonderful truth about our precious and complex race: that humility and ideological incompletion are *meant* to be a wonderful part of our human nature that should and can be celebrated rather than feared. One of the experiences I have been most helped, challenged and changed by, resulted from me making one of the wisest and most crucial decisions of my life and first submitting myself to systemic Psychotherapy.

In one session, my long-suffering therapist and I were discussing issues of personal and societal belief and I was expressing my frustration at the conditionality of some of my experiences, while he discussed his own faith in relation to his extensive Psychotherapeutic training. He suddenly became thoughtful and then tenderly looked at me and with such peacefulness said gently;

"*I find that my own faith works best in the context of uncertainty.*'

I suddenly found myself quietly weeping.

It is a weeping that continues in my heart for the very many that I have seen damaged so profoundly by the imposition of someone else's decreed ideological *certainty* about their lives and identities, and the consequential catastrophic emotional and spiritual consequences.

I was filled with wonder and awe at what had been so simply expressed but that can never be allowed in dogmatic and regimented upbringings or societal contexts, in which certainty is absolutely required – where doubt or questioning are called *dangerous* and rendered synonymous with weakness and shame.

In such environments, many fragile and naturally explorative individuals suffer long years spent in agonising internal struggles that are entirely unnecessary.

Surely, what a wonderful freedom we are able to live out when we stop trying to convince others that our insecurely held views are the only 'truth' and rather hold them in integrity, passionately, but in the courage that our position is simply one of *faith* in things that are ultimately unknown.

And that this is not only wholly acceptable but that it works perfectly, whatever our chosen position. Only in this revelation and bravery, can all of us co-exist with one another in harmony, growth and mutual respect.

I was recently reading a wonderful and profound memoir by a lifelong religious and community leader, who in later life has become increasingly agnostic.

After more than 50 years of extensive involvement at every level of leadership of a popular societal religion, he remarked that it was a deeply damaging and misguided perspective within religious thought that the opposite of faith is *doubt* and that such a view has been so widely expressed to berate those who *question*. In truth and reality he exclaims, *the exact opposite of true and living faith… is certainty*.

True faith *must* leave room for *wonder, mystery and most of all humility*, or it is not faith at all but prideful fanaticism, that great murderous curse of human history.

However, clearly it is not only those ideologically or religiously motivated who appear to suffer from the tendency to regularly browbeat their opponents and critics into a guilt-ridden and psychological pulp when it comes to differences of opinion.

In fact, despite what we might read and imagine, we would be wise to see that it is simply an astoundingly indelible trait within human nature and not primarily an ideological one around opinion.

I read a particular newspaper in order to be challenged and am often shocked by the thinly disguised venom meted out by scientifically orientated thinkers who describe themselves as liberal, on those so bold as to suggest that their take on explorative science does not have all the answers.

Increasingly, I hear such self-proclaimed 'enlightened' thinkers pouring vociferous derision on anyone suggesting that even that most pure of thought disciplines, science, has to occasionally employ an element of theorisation in that which is ultimately unprovable around life's big questions.

While some with whom I have discussed these things may feel that the perspectives I am describing are actually the exception and not the rule, and consequently it is fair to say that I may be over-simplifying the polemics involved, I find that from my reading about world affairs to regular mentoring of individual people, that intensely narrow and fanatical views seem to me ever more prevalent in many parts of our society and modern world.

Sadly such attitudes do not appear to be on the wane in man's complex and unstable relationship with himself.

Surely, it would be such a wonderful thing for us as a human family should we find ourselves finally able to consider that whatever our view or perspective, if we have true integrity, we must be courageous enough to recognise that in so many areas and in so many places our perceived knowledge of many of life's fundamental and contentious questions is still woefully incomplete.

Consequently, individual views might best be held with grace and gentleness and with a commitment to avoid conflict and celebrate tolerance and dignity rather than our certainties used as a loaded gun trained on all those ignorant enough to disagree with us.

I hope that we might think about these things and let them gracefully touch our thoughts.

We *all* need change, and can *all* benefit from adjustment in the humble recognition that the distant sound of grace is soothing.

Its gentle tide is a welcome sound to us all.

Humility vs Judgment

The whole problem with the world is that fools and fanatics are always so certain of themselves, and wiser people so full of doubts.

Bertrand Russell

I would like to expand and continue on the exploration of this theme by looking deeper into what I believe is the crucial issue of human judgmentalism.

Whether we are aware of its power in our lives or not, the judgments that we make and the way in which we make them is an immensely important issue and unless our understanding and appropriation of personal judgment is fully mature, any awareness we may have accrued will be completely corrupted in both ourselves and in others.

While there is nothing that can be more life-giving and healthy than a person judging their own soul in *wisdom, truth and love,* conversely there is perhaps nothing more destructive, than an undisciplined orientation towards the inappropriate and unbridled judgment of either oneself, or of another person.

What then is a judgment?

It is the practice of making a value decision about another person or situation from the confines and limitations of one's *own personal perspective*. Effectively, we are imparting *our* opinion or worldview on someone or something else.

However, it is extremely important to say that the ability and will to make judgments is entirely appropriate and necessary in life and the responsibility and courage to do so is an essential part of our humanity if we are to be whole and live well.

We must make judgments on who will be our friends or partners and spouses, where we will live, what we will do with our time and an enormous range of other issues as we navigate life's uncertain tides. Furthermore, our judgments may be consistently affirming and kind to those around us and we may build others in love and encouragement. If this is the case then our words will be the means by which many will be encouraged and blessed and we possess a wonderful and rare gift.

But there is a point at which our *negative* judgments on others – if unbridled and undisciplined – can become incredibly toxic to others in their wellbeing and spiritual walk towards awareness and health.

Amongst the numerous cases I have seen of hurt inflicted upon the human soul, the worst damage I have witnessed has always been revealed in the psyches of those inappropriately *judged* whilst at a vulnerable stage of life by unwise parents, authority figures or by a toxic combination of both.

Now it is very important to say at this point that negative and scarring judgment only occurs in the context of the judging person's *certainty about what they see in their victim.*

And judgmental certainty is a really very interesting issue.

Indeed, of all the countless cases of violence, and abuse that I have seen, what is the one factor I have found most regularly linking the perpetrators, despite a great range of completely diverse individuals and situations?

It is this: that so very many of such perpetrators are ultimately revealed to be *unable to question their own behaviour.*

They are invariably absolutely *certain* that they are beyond reproach, and that what they are doing is wholly acceptable, regardless of any cost to their victims.

On a wider level, it is interesting that historically, we find that many of the individuals revealed to be most evil throughout the centuries were always utterly *convinced of the certainty* of the *rightness* of their actions, regardless of the staggering damage and enormous human cost.

I often think on these things to challenge myself about the very real and perilous nature of judgment and personal certainty – in particular, my own remarkably prevalent daily habit of judgment upon countless other people and issues.

Interestingly, judgmental people who are often heard to judge their spouses, peers, children or colleagues tend on the whole to be angry, insecure, and unhappy people; and it is always their own innate dissatisfaction that propels them to look outward towards others, identify supposed failings and then make inappropriate and critical judgments.

I wonder if this is because the judgment of others provides a welcome psychological diversion from the discontent that they barely even recognise to be present in their limited self-perception. All of us will have known people who are fundamentally embittered, and who are constantly doing down others to make themselves feel better. Such people are so often deeply lonely, unhappy, psychologically traumatised and insecure individuals.

In contrast, people who are healthy, happy and well-adjusted tend to make many less judgments on others – in fact their energy for judging people is normally reserved for their own self-censure which is often only carried out tentatively, patiently and with prior careful thought.

Deeply emotive and negative judgmental outbursts on another soul can be profoundly toxic and dangerous. But the most poisonous of all judgmental behaviours is what I will call ideological or fanatical judgmentalism.

I want to offer some examples; variations of which I have heard regularly in numerous situations with clients over the years:

An adolescent and sensitive teenager is told that black people possess a slightly inferior IQ, but are naturally better athletes.

A vulnerable teenager is advised that she better not pursue a career as a pilot because she is better suited 'to a more feminine job.'

A successful scientist tells their student that spirituality or faith of any kind is stupidity and the worst kind of ignorance.

A father tells their adolescent son who is negotiating a burgeoning sexuality that 'gays are pathetic'.

A family member tells their 8-year-old relative that she will always be 'fat'.

A religious teacher tells a child that masturbation is evil and leads straight to sin and Hell.

A parent tell their young son that his other parent and main carer is 'a bad parent and doesn't love him properly'.

I know that I need not explain why such judgments and countless pronouncements in the same vein, expressed relentlessly by ignorant people, are so very seriously damaging and dangerous and the cause of such immense destruction.

Whatever our position, we simply must open our eyes to the realisation that the worst and most serious kind of negative judgment is that which imposes an abstract paradigm or standard that really only exists in anger and fear within the mind of the judging party, but through their words and actions is inflicted upon the hearer to their great trauma and detriment. There is almost nothing that is more perilous than such pronouncements to the tenderness and beauty of a human soul.

This occurs because the psyche – that in order to function healthily requires confidence and love – inevitably becomes scarred and traumatised and is then often overcome by the same fear, darkness and lack of innate security as the judging party.

In particular these things seem to occur most regularly when such behaviours and conclusions are inherited, and the hearer is evermore gradually infected with the darkness and toxicity of the judgmental mind of the person ministering negativity directly onto them.

Although I only want to touch upon a brief and perhaps simplistic overview of what I am aware is an extremely complex subject, I hope that we can consider the immense importance of keeping our negative judgments of our loved ones and fellow humans to a minimum. We need be painfully aware of the propensity for our own ideological fears and hang-ups to reproduce deep trauma and damage in others, even if we genuinely believe that we are simply 'instructing' them.

Fear and negativity is seldom an effective instrument for inculcating good in our pupils, children, spouses or colleagues. Instead it tends to give birth to subtle and yet deep psychological damage within the psyche of those upon whom it is inflicted.

Let us think upon these truths soberly, for our own sakes, and for others.

Finally, what may help us to become less judgmental either outwardly or simply in our hearts and our minds, is our willingness to consider that we are often particularly gentle and forgiving of *ourselves* over the course of our complex and challenging lives.

Within just a few days – if we are aware and diligent enough to listen to our own souls, we will likely witness a bewildering array of unpalatable behaviours and orientations: un-kindnesses, jealousies, lusts; and an ongoing covetousness for that which is not ours.

With this in mind, if only we can try to extend the same relentless forgiveness and mercy that we continually afford *ourselves* to our neighbours and those that we may leap to judge whether inwardly or vocally, we might find ourselves able to quiet the deeply human judgmental streak in our hearts and behaviours.

Furthermore we should consider that so very often, the meagre speck that provokes such outrage when noticed in our brother's eye, may well be obscured by the log we carry in our own that only becomes evident when we are willing to peer into the mirror.

When and if we *do* feel impelled to administer judgment, we must also be aware and brave enough to only communicate a standard of rationale in our feelings by which we would be willing to be held accountable to *ourselves*.

These two final principles may serve as the best yardsticks by which we can increasingly become masters of our own souls (and more pertinently, mouths!) on these perilous and sensitive issues.

Certainly, we can learn from the centuries-old wisdom conveyed therein.

As we are willing to do so, we may perhaps discover ourselves becoming a means of blessing to others rather than the bringer of a curse; an instrument of healing and mercy rather than a cause of harm, and someone in whom the power and propensity to bind up rather than to tear down, is made manifest in great and life-giving beauty.

Uniqueness and Difference

Over these many years, I have been privileged to work extremely closely with a diverse range of individuals and groups within a context of intimacy; persistently exploring those very deepest feelings, secrets, hopes and fears.

In this practice, the enormous amount that we discover about our human *uniqueness* as diverse individuals never ceases to thrill and amaze me.

Though we may be physiologically, culturally and to outward appearances relatively similar, if only we are patient and curious we soon discover overwhelmingly that we are all so very different.

What is revelation to one appears folly to another, what is light to one is complete darkness to another, what is incomprehensible to *us* may be perfect and life giving clarity to our neighbour. Furthermore, we are not only so different as separate thinkers but we are also wildly diverse in our experiences, perspectives, views and attitudes.

Given this truth, I find myself regularly surprised by how often we as people seem rather than to *recognise and embrace* this individualism, to ignore it for the sake of ease and security.

This is not necessarily wholly our fault: clearly, our cultural and educative systems impart a considerable pigeonholing that starts from birth and functions like a great relentless harvester of individuals in nearly every human society and culture.

Such social categorisation is the main culprit in consigning us to limiting boxes, but sadly many of us inhabit them gladly in the mistaken hope that behind a 'label' there is a sincere identity and some precious security.

Instead, and if we are to ever be truly aware and free we must be willing to embrace and to trust our uniqueness and as a consequence, be *brave enough* to inhabit our whole souls, and then courageously live life as the *main character in our own story*.

Furthermore, although there are some obvious exceptions in parts of the world, increasingly we have more freedom and power to govern ourselves and lives than we have ever had throughout human history. I wonder though if in a very real sense that it is a freedom that few of us have even begun to really embrace and consider.

And one factor why I find this particular question *so* compelling is this:

I have both worked with and known people from the most appallingly neglected and abused backgrounds who despite all, have achieved tremendous healing and health, vibrancy and recovery. And yet I have known so many others who have had a relatively supported background and much less trauma but whose lives are almost unbelievably chaotic and whose souls are the most lost.

Why?

Why is this the case?

Why is it that some individuals take full responsibility to rise from the most appalling circumstances and achieve deep and life-giving awareness and the resulting wonder, and yet others who have often suffered little by comparison, show no sign or hope of realising and facing truth about their state or finding what is a profoundly elusive sense of wholeness and wellbeing?

Clearly there are multiple studies, books and conclusions written around this subject and definitely many complex reasons for such phenomena.

I must stress that the underlying reasons and factors *are* indeed complex and I hesitate to be overly simplistic in discussing them.

But in the next chapters I would like to illuminate one particular element that I have come to believe is immensely important in our exploration of true awareness and personal transformation.

For now, let me briefly conclude by returning to our central theme with one final eloquent expression from Desmond Tutu that I hope we will find thought-provoking and inspiring to mediate upon as we continue our journey:

'Differences are not intended to separate, to alienate.

We are different precisely in order to realise our need of one another'.

What a wonderful perspective to inhabit in our hearts and minds.

Perhaps we will see such wisdom increasingly permeate our society.

We have never needed it more.

Human Will and Redemption

I am not a product of my circumstances.
I am a product of my decisions.

Stephen Covey

To introduce the themes ahead, I will begin by making a bold statement and then attempt to qualify and explain its meaning.

It has always seemed to me such a profoundly significant truth – the consequences of which are so far-reaching for us all:

The extent to which an individual will become truly aware in their life and achieve genuine growth is entirely proportionate to the extent to which that individual will take responsibility for their own will.

We can only really understand the tremendous import of this phenomenon when we first consider the considerable number of people in the world who consider themselves victims of consequence and think of themselves as such through the course of their lives. Now to be very clear: *I am not talking about the genuine sufferers of the many countless undeserved horrors that blight our fragile humanity such as poverty, disability, bereavement, severe illness or the relational abuse of the vulnerable.*

Clearly, there are some appalling and indiscriminate burdens that individuals and families must bear in this great struggle of human life. I don't know why this is the case. I do not understand.

These things are incomprehensible if we try to explain, rationalise or categorise them and our only sincere response must be humble sadness and a deep empathy.

Some things that are suffered in our broken world by the innocent simply must not be spoken of by those of us who have been fortunate enough to avoid them.

We should simply remain silent and mourn and nothing else is appropriate.

But it is also true that a very large proportion of challenges and difficulties that so many of us must face are actually linked entirely to our own *responses* to life, our *choices* and the way in which we choose to employ and utilise our innate will. The greatest desire and goal of a wise and sincere teacher or healer of any kind, will be to tenaciously attempt to imbue the human mind and heart of their subject both with acceptance of themselves, but also with the revelation that in fact, invariably in our complex lives, a staggering and often entirely untapped level and amount of power *lies with us* and we are not simply the victims of circumstance and chance.

In truth, so often, we have immense and lifelong power over our own destinies *if we simply take responsibility for our own will and begin to use it in wisdom and discipline.*

When an individual finally embraces this truth and then willingly works to harness, direct and utilise such willpower on a daily basis to bring change and healing, the greatest power they may ever witness and experience will be unleashed.

Suddenly, immense and lasting change becomes possible.

Problems that seemed insurmountable before are rendered entirely conquerable.

The exhilarating dawn of a new life appears on the horizon.

There is certainly no joy and adventure anywhere else in all of life quite like the realisation and beauty of this seldom embarked upon journey.

But it is a hard, hard thing to face and we must not be flippant about the tremendous battle that rages in a human heart on a daily basis between the simple desire to submit to things as they are; blaming circumstance, other people or our background for our sadness and cursing our bad fortune – or the rare phenomenon of those who utterly refuse such a position and admit that regardless of where they find themselves, *ultimate power still lies with them.*

Louis L'Amour puts it like this: *'There comes a time when it lies within a man's grasp to shape the clay of his life into the sort of thing he wishes to be. Only the weak blame parents, the times, lack of good fortune, or quirks of fate.'*

Many of the greatest minds throughout history arrived at this wonderful conclusion and in its revelation released the power in themselves necessary to achieve their world changing contributions, often in context of incredible suffering.

Nelson Mandela cites such a life-changing experience in which he was given the extraordinary poem about human will, 'Invictus' by William Ernest Henley. He read and memorised these words, reciting them constantly within, to strengthen and focus his soul throughout the long years of his torturous incarceration.

Henley describes these profound truths so beautifully in verse:

Out of the night that covers me,
Black as the Pit from pole to pole,
I thank whatever gods may be
For my unconquerable soul.

In the fell clutch of circumstance
I have not winced nor cried aloud.
Under the bludgeonings of chance
My head is bloody, but unbowed.

Beyond this place of wrath and tears
Looms but the Horror of the shade,
And yet the menace of the years
Finds, and shall find, me unafraid.

It matters not how strait the gate,
How charged with punishments the scroll.
I am the master of my fate:
I am the captain of my soul.

You see, *I* am the captain of my soul.

And *you* are the captain of yours.

It is impossible to exaggerate how often humans fear, reject and will flee from this great truth *at all costs* and sometimes for an entire lifetime.

Though we so very often have ultimate power in our innate will to influence, change and to a great extent control our daily destiny and quality of life, we commonly absolutely refuse to consider, admit and face such responsibility.

We blithely blame our partners, our parents, God, our backgrounds and an enormous range of other factors for our condition, attributing ultimate power to them, when instead we must courageously face the truth that it is in our response to such things that power is made manifest for and through us.

It is much easier and more comfortable to deny the enormous consequential inevitability of decisions that *we have made and can still make ourselves, and the lifelong consequences thereof.* We often choose to rather think of ourselves as victims.

Consequentially, so many of us are ultimately angry with others, with the world or with God, unhappy, disappointed and frustrated with our lives and relationships and an enormous amount of individuals feel trapped in dynamics that *we tell ourselves are not and have not been of our own choosing.*

It is convenient to feel powerless and weak, and that we do not have the means necessary to shape our destiny.

Many of us would much rather rest in our own perceived inadequacy, disappointment and victimhood and be left alone there to live out disappointed lives in which we think of ourselves as victims in some cosmologically unkind game.

But this is a lie that must be bravely faced, stared down and utterly overcome.

Though we may fear it, we must be courageous, and be willing to face the truth, a truth described beautifully by Marianne Williamson:

'*Our deepest fear is not that we are inadequate.*

Our deepest fear is that we are powerful beyond measure.

It is our light, not our darkness that most frightens us. We ask ourselves,

Who am I to be brilliant, gorgeous, talented, fabulous?

Actually, who are you not to be?

You are a child of God.

Your playing small does not serve the world.

There is nothing enlightened about shrinking so that other people won't feel insecure around you.

We are all meant to shine, as children do.

We were born to make manifest the glory of God that is within us.

It's not just in some of us; it's in everyone.

And as we let our own light shine, we unconsciously give other people permission to do the same.

As we are liberated from our own fear, our presence automatically liberates others.'

Human Labelling and Healing

*The only person you are destined to become
is the person you decide to be.*

Ralph Waldo Emerson

These things are challenging to consider.

Certainly, our lives are paradoxical, complex and I want to do my best to avoid being glib about such momentous things.

But I think that they are profoundly important.

I hope now to move on to some further thoughts about human will and the identities we take upon ourselves.

As we are talking about awareness, change and the over-coming of our wounds, we may recognise that we all live in a time and a society in which people are generally de-scribed in clearly defined categories, under labels and so very often as helpless and hapless victims of their unfor-tunate circumstance. 'He's an alcoholic', or 'she has mental health issues', 'she is anorexic' or 'he's unemployed'.

We seem to hear such unfortunate phrases relentlessly used in conversation to describe individuals, colleagues, friends and family members on a regular basis.

And tragically what this state of affairs has created within fragile human psyches, is the culture that so many of us now inhabit – a culture in which so very often, our identity is defined solely by what we have been through, often manifested by our failings and troubles or simply by other folks' labelled perceptions of us despite them seeing a woefully incomplete picture of our souls and true identities.

Truly, we all see *'through a glass, darkly'* (1 Corinthians) and we would do well to be more wisely circumspect before we put such labels onto our complex and beautiful fellow souls.

And yet such wise and generous human dignity appears rare in our modern age of 'progress'.

As discussed in previous chapters, many humans suffer from a particularly judgmental streak linked to their innate human insecurity, and despite often doing so unaware, pigeonhole others in order to create their cherished but incomplete personal sense of knowledgeable security.

But the considerable danger, as I have seen over many years in a great range of different individuals, is that people very often *come to see themselves and their innate identities, as a function of their backgrounds and pasts and the labels that others attach to them.*

Furthermore, while background and upbringing certainly constitute such a considerable informer of identity and wellbeing for better or for worse, a small percentage of people that I have known and worked with, completely refuse this paradigm and demand that their identity and destiny rest entirely upon their *responses* to what they have been through and not the cards dealt to them by circumstance.

I can't tell you what an immense privilege and remarkable phenomenon it is to witness such people addressing their problems and wounds without self-pity, bitterness or blame.

Instead, they seem established in the complete assurance that regardless of the ill done to them and life's many challenges, *it is they and only they who are ultimately responsible for their condition and future.*

However painful and long the process, they are certain that they can entirely take back control of their destiny achieving healing and wholeness.

This rare condition in people is always both truly remarkable and deeply humbling to see in its immense beauty and power.

But the most profound and moving and wonderful reality about this phenomenon is that unlike so many others these individuals generally and overwhelmingly do achieve their true healing and do succeed in deciding their own destinies.

However long it takes, and whatever the cost, regularly:

They do.

Through a marvellous commitment to awareness and change, there are those who bravely overcome the most momentous issues regardless of whether they have suffered abandonment, severe abuse, an incredible array of challenges or simply the deep suffering caused by inherited mental health or physical issues.

It is likely that you too may know just such a person and that they have inspired and amazed you.

One of the great privileges of my life has been to watch such remarkable people quietly turn from their wounded or damaged imposed identities and by sheer force of will and relentless determination, carve out a completely new life for themselves and achieve the optimum measure of health of which they are capable, finding happy relationships and embodying responsible parenting when the time comes.

It is almost like such individuals innately have a special knowledge and sense that so many of the rest of us fail to possess in our attachment to labelling and the resulting perceived security of our 'victimhood'.

Such individuals seem to be able to trust and then obediently follow at a much greater pace than the rest of us, the great voice of love and truth within that whispers to them that they are not merely a label and need not be defined by the wrong done to them, but that it can be utterly overcome.

I would like to explore some of the characteristics, commitments and behaviours that I have witnessed in these people as their stories have unfolded.

How is it that they are willing and able to take responsibility for their own will, their life, decisions and destiny and achieve remarkable growth?

And by what means?

Grace

*I do not at all understand the mystery of Grace –
Only that it meets us where we are but does not leave us
where it found us.*

Anne Lamott

I want to continue with a discussion of the factors that make the deeply aware people I have described, *different* in terms of the way they find genuine truth and then act upon their knowledge in a way that is so powerful in their lives.

I also want to make clear that instead of sensationalising or mystifying such people and behaviours, it is my belief and certainly my experience and intention that we can all aspire to and achieve the traits if only we are willing to be humble and brave.

Surely none of us are so far lost that we are immune to the call of such glorious and life-giving possibilities.

We are all of us a work in progress and are all utterly capable of complete change if only we are willing to listen and to learn.

It is this belief alone that has propelled and sustained me on the lonely and frustrating journey of writing about these peculiar issues despite the constant temptation to give up in the face of clumsy prose, laziness and the ongoing discovery of so many deep weaknesses within my own soul and behaviours.

Amazingly, I find that regardless of these cloying things, I am *still* strugglingly attempting this difficult book because I have to my great surprise and joy come to discover that even someone as stubborn and as proud as myself can learn to explore, listen, and then learn... if only I am willing and curious.

I am certainly one of the most difficult, self-obsessed, judgmental and selfish people I know.

And yet, *even I am able to achieve real and profound change.*

What then, are the factors that underpin those most remarkable and aware individuals as they pursue their true healing – the themes that we must surely all attempt to learn and consider if we are to walk in the footsteps towards true awareness and lasting change?

The first must surely be: *Forgiveness.*

I have noticed that in each and every individual that I have witnessed overcome the most tragic circumstances, not one is overly interested and concerned with anger, bitterness, blame or revenge pertaining to their sufferings.

Make no mistake; these individuals are brave enough to face and then acknowledge the wrong done to them and also to willingly address failure on their own part. But once this necessary process has been navigated, they will – as soon as is humanly possible – pursue forgiveness of themselves, their tormentors and of any others involved. Such people invariably possess a deep orientation towards and an ability to *forgive*.

They do not choose to blame themselves or others for their predicament and instead simply look forward and refuse to spend further energy or emotional resources on finding fault, despite the genuine and natural justice that this might embody to others.

Even when forgiveness is a long and arduous and agonising process, they persist.

In the end, such persistence renders them utterly free.

Perhaps most interestingly, I have discovered that Forgiveness is actually at root a *boundaries* issue. When individuals can see beyond themselves and believe in a purpose and a reality that is *greater than them*selves, they are able to completely forgive. This is partly why in his ground-breaking and enormously influential work, Joseph Campbell describes the hero as someone who lives for something 'bigger than oneself.'

Tragically, if instead a person's own feelings and certainty are at the centre of their orientation, forgiveness and peace will never be possible and their lives will be cursed by relational difficulty, conflict and daily drama of which they will always consider themselves the victim.

There is a sublime quote about this phenomenon by James Baldwin who remarked: *'I imagine one of the reasons people cling to their hates so stubbornly is because they sense, once hate is gone, they will be forced to deal with pain.'*

I have barely ever met a person who has ongoing issues with anger and inappropriate emotional responses that is not su-pressing deep pain of which they are often too ashamed and frightened to confront.

And crucially: this is where courage comes in to human life, and is such an absolutely essential component of in-ner-healing: *Only the brave achieve redemption, because the most courageous act a human can ever undertake is to face reality within*, and then undertake *whatever* is necessary to overcome that which threatens their entire relational existence. I person-ally furthermore believe in something I have challenged many passion filled and idealistic young people with whom it has been my privilege to work: *the most subversive and pow-erful act you will ever do in the whole world, is to commit to the redemption and healing of your soul.*

I have seen the most inspiring and remarkable of people of all ages, decide on such a path; and then use the ability that I will highlight next, to cling to it against the constant temptation to flee the pain of awakening and slip back into delusional oblivion and victimhood.

Persistence. This great gift seems to enable individuals to somehow keep striving rather than to ever give up their claim to a better and happier future in which their healing is made manifest. Even in the darkest times and despite sporadic wobbles of confidence and the occasional loneliness of tears, they simply refuse to stop and surrender. *They will not*. Instead, they simply keep going: on and on and on and on and on... until they are free. Winston Churchill famously said: 'Success is not final, failure is not fatal: it is the courage to continue that counts.'

As we continue, truly changing people possess a strong orientation towards an attitude of complexity, integrity and the corresponding wise rejection of well-meaning contributions from those I will call The 'Explainers'.

Rather than accept trite explanations for their own condition and background, they are unwilling to allow simplistic conclusions to provide sole context to their core issues and circumstances.

They accept their own brokenness and yet remain explorative, curious, open minded and seem to maintain a quiet responsibility in themselves rather than employing an ideological or 'explanatory' rhetoric that would make them the subject of a societal or supernatural game in which they are immediately cast by others as the victim and/or hero.

Unfortunately, many of those whom I have worked with have been seduced by being told that their very real childhood traumas can be prescribed instant healing and closure via integration into political, social or religious fundamentalism of any kind.

They are told that if only *'they believe the right thing'* – then this ideological certainty renders them to be an entirely reformed person and that those things with which they have struggled will no longer exist.

Inevitably such people are instructed in no uncertain terms to follow a prescriptive set of life rules and promised such rules will ensure their complete safety and health. Effectively they are put upon a kind of tightrope that *reality and their natural paradoxical humanity renders slippery.*

It doesn't take much discernment to see that the trouble with such simplistic teaching turns out to be its denial and complete misunderstanding of the *two very real* sides of the clear paradox inherent within human weaknesses: certainly, we *can* overcome and transcend our past and leave it behind us and in one respect letting go should be encouraged and endorsed – but simultaneously we must be brave enough to constantly acknowledge where we have come from and that our failings and our history must be courageously faced over a lifetime in order to continually overcome its negative power, by painstakingly bringing the crucial issues into the light.

This process happens best in a humble, gradual, painstaking persistence, pursued openly in naked accountability to our loved and trusted fellow travellers.

This concept is described beautifully in the sentence; *'If we say we have no sin, we deceive ourselves and the truth is not in us.'*

Without this foundation, in all of the cases in which I have seen such basic over-simplification of the human condition, ironically individuals are in fact imbuing their suppressed and hidden wounds with a much greater power by pretending that they no longer exist.

This is a very concerning imbalance because what commonly happens – despite the trusting sincerity on the part of the willing hearer – is that past undesirable traits and orientations *do* of course naturally reappear at times. Rather than being gently and truthfully faced and acknowledged in ongoing accountability, they are hidden carefully or explained away, consigning the sufferer to a lifetime of struggle against duplicitous practice, the great tension and guilt thereof causing in their own soul a great wound.

Instead, and if they are people of a sincere, mature and rounded relationship with themselves, the gifted use their conviction to propel them towards the constant pursuit of openness and the deeply held principle that instead of fanatically seeking answers and asking *why* they have suffered, they seem to trust quietly.

Entirely regardless of their individual orientation – they believe that they are protected, loved and nurtured by a force beyond and yet within and around them in which they simply trust. They seem able to trust that even despite its great darkness, the world has the propensity to be a safe and healing place.

When such trust and integrity is honoured and transfigured like this, I have noticed that it often becomes immensely beautiful, bearing much fruit in others.

The people involved humbly demonstrate a clear example of that supreme and eternal principle that the 'truth *will* set free'.

They believe deeply that they need not ever run from nor fear this truth, however painful and challenging, because they fundamentally trust that they are valued and accepted.

Gratitude. The gratefulness of those who achieve true freedom, even in the most appalling, challenging and dire circumstances, is wonderful and remarkable to see. Such individuals look for and focus upon the 'silver lining in the cloud', and when they find it, are thankful and satisfied. They carefully reject society's remarkable notion of entitlement and expected privilege, instead being thankful for the simplest things.

On a daily or hourly basis they learn to count their blessings and think about what they *do* have and what they can simply be grateful for.

This orientation, perhaps more than any other, appears again and again in the most psychologically and spiritually healthy of humans, ensuring their ability to be truly happy and to experience real joy despite life's challenges and difficulty.

Accountability. The most deeply aware tend to be unwilling to pursue their journey of exploration and healing in isolation. They pursue intimacy with others in which they share nakedly rather than craving affirmation and respect through shallow pretence. Often, the content of their relational pursuits is a mutual deep questioning of their own motives and orientations in partnership with their fellow travellers.

They have no secrets that have not been shared – no skeletons in their cupboards. And in fact, eventually it is truthful to say that they generally end up having no cupboards.

They are real with everyone, without fear or need for self-preservation; even when such honesty is rejected by the self-righteous who find it unbearably discomforting.

They have the confidence and security to simply be themselves.

This seems to give them a resilience and a life within.

In conclusion, it is important to close by saying what may appear most obvious in this discussion; that trait which is in fact most important of all:

The truly brave amongst us approach inner change and transformation as a sacred friend; a friend that they do not in the least bit fear, but that in fact they seek a constantly evolving deeper intimacy with.

They view life as a great adventure; they are brave and willing in recognising their own deep need, and they recognise that most profound of all truths: *that external change in our lives is only possible after internal change of our hearts made manifest in humility and discipline.*

Perhaps of all the attitudes in those that I have walked with over these years, it is *this* rare orientation that is the most astoundingly powerful and life-giving of all.

I will write more about this beautiful light in Part 2, but I would like to end this section now and come back to such principles later.

But let us remember that *we are each the main character in our own story.*

It is an entirely unique story and one that can only be written – for good or for ill – *by us and by no-one else.*

Either we will shrink back from this momentous task and merely live an existence of disempowered victimhood, buffeted by the winds of fortune and fate, or we will place our shoulders to the plough day after day and push on bravely; determined to author our own furrow of destiny.

We certainly cannot control life, and at times must suffer illness, tragedy or misfortune.

But unless we recognise the astounding power made manifest through our responses to life's events, we are missing the greatest adventure we will ever embark upon during our short time on this beautiful planet.

Though our family, friends or peers may seek to tell us who and what we are and how the world is, *ultimate power about who we will be, lies within us.*

This awesome power does not leave us until our final breath.

Whether we will accept it or not, *we* hold the key within to decide whom we will serve.

The more we become brave and take full responsibility for our own responses, actions, attitudes and their inevitable results, the more we will recognise our own power and become increasingly whole.

And let us be grateful that if only we have eyes to see, we will recognise remarkable fellow travellers from whom we can learn much.

In our struggles along the thirsty stretches of dry track, may we reach across to grasp an outstretched hand and stumble together along this rocky road towards awareness.

In journeying together, we may happen upon gentle and calm oases that were previously invisible.

Awareness and Self-Nurture

Self-care is not selfish or self-indulgent. We cannot nurture others from a dry well. We need to take care of our own needs first, then we can give from our surplus.

Jennifer Louden

I have talked a little about other people, human will and what we may learn and gather from others on the road.

I want to continue now by looking at awareness in the context of the integral self-love discussed previously.

Regardless of others, how do we as individuals walk in a way that through our actions and behaviours, exemplifies and inculcates a truly loving awareness of ourselves? How can we consistently and tenaciously live our lives to afford ourselves the maximum propensity for healing and wholeness?

We have talked about how we must learn to self-nurture; to tend to that garden of our souls and to make this our absolute priority. Indeed, without this crucial discipline, we will find that we are simply unable to truly love those precious to us because we can only give that which we have received and has been made manifest within.

The well of our own heart must be kept flowing and deep, or we will find ourselves drained and arid when the time comes for our desire to water and feed our loved ones.

What then must we do to dig and cultivate a fresh flowing source of life within?

In the same way that our bodies require regular sustenance in order to perform in the way that we want them to, our souls require feeding if they are to contain the life and vitality essential for a greater awareness, the essential pursuit of change and goodness in our relationships with others.

The basic parallels of diet equalling performance between management of our physical appetite and the nurture of our inner wellbeing hold absolutely true. The world is the way that it has always been, and the simple truth cannot be escaped: what we invest will generally be what we harvest; we will 'reap that which we sow'.

Whether we want to become an athlete or if we hope to build muscle tone, if we want to lose weight or hope to gain it, we must carefully nurture our bodies and be mindful about what we put into them or all our efforts will be undermined. In the case of our souls, the same is absolutely true. What we choose to do, watch, read and expose our hearts and minds to will surely yield a harvest within us either for our good or for ill.

It is remarkable how many people each day, each hour, suffer relational anguish, depression or anxiety, oblivious that the root cause of their psychological malaise is down to what they have prioritised and consumed with their mind and time – what has become their spiritual diet.

Consequently, it is almost impossible to even begin to heal such affliction without investigating a person's psychological intake with the same care and attention that we naturally employ to seek to improve their physicality.

Mental and emotional healing is only ever possible through a willingness in us as individuals to learn to *reflect* on our habits, our thought processes and what we are giving attention to, and then for us to be humble and willing enough to experiment with new perspectives and change. However, in our human immaturity – and just as we do physically – many of us want to continue to consume exactly what we desire at the moment we wish for it, and still fully expect to avoid any negative consequence.

Furthermore and seemingly increasingly, a great deal of people are now using inappropriate medication, porn, extremely unhealthy or even illegal drugs and a dizzying range of perceived shortcuts to try to circumnavigate the consequences of individually held responsibility for the careful management of their psychological and physical appetites.

Unfortunately, as time goes on and life follows its inevitable path, the results of such attempts tragically prove both irreversible and catastrophic.

There is overwhelming evidence that the only true health we can attain is that which flows from tenacious discipline. True wellbeing is always holistic and truly integrative between mind, body and soul. Such health requires commitment and patience. In the words of Nietzsche: 'The essential thing in heaven and earth is that there should be *long obedience in the same direction*. There thereby results and has always resulted, in something which has made life worth living.'

From a psychological and spiritual perspective, if only we can discover and then regularly prioritise a healthy intake of that which nourishes and blesses our souls and soothes our minds, we will reap a tremendous harvest and avoid much unnecessary fatigue and heartache. This process is complex and inevitably takes *time* to discover just what it is that is good for us and that truly *feeds* us.

Additionally, life is seasonal and there are a great many stages in which time to invest in ourselves is not only scarce but only comes when we are exhausted and utterly bereft of emotional and psychological resources.

And this is OK.

It is ludicrous to imagine that a father or mother with young children, a busy job and large house can drop their responsibilities at any moment to concentrate on their inner wellbeing.

But despite such basic and obvious truth, it is also true to recognise that: the ones of us having to give the most, need the most to find those rare times of peace in which we can be nurtured and replenished in order that we can carry on in a healthy way.

Furthermore, the fact remains and must be always repeated, that generally, as our lives progress and more is required of us in a family, job or relational situation we can only give that which we have accepted and received within – that which has been made manifest in our own hearts, or we will find ourselves pouring from an empty cup.

Self-nurture requires us to prioritise investment in caring spiritually for ourselves. The diligent practice required, wonderfully results in us becoming increasingly aware and able to wisely and regularly care spiritually for ourselves and maintain our inner-health.

This skill is certainly not something that comes naturally or indeed that we are normally taught and brought up to do.

Despite being the most essential element of establishing and maintaining human wisdom, remarkably few of us are ever taught or shown how to self-nurture and even fewer of us experience what it is like to witness our parents exemplifying these skills to us.

Invariably, individuals in each generation consider themselves to have received insufficient nurture from parents who were unaware of how to invest in their own psycho-spiritual awareness, let alone their children!

If and when this is the case, we must wisely understand the tremendous cultural differences in our parent's upbringing and generational backgrounds and utterly *forgive* them.

This act of will is by no means easy or simple. But it is absolutely necessary and essential to life.

The inability to understand and forgive in this crucial regard, will not only severely inhibit our own growth but will mean we invariably remain trapped in a state of paralysis, smarting from our own historical upsets and hurts rather than choosing the warmth, acceptance and grace that is both necessary and fully available, in order to begin a journey towards wholeness and freedom.

We must face, accept, forgive and then let go.

There is no other way.

Forgiveness is certainly one of the hardest of all awareness truths to live out and one that demands a much greater discussion.

For now, let us simply be willing to consider that some of us may even today have the chance of a new start – a new beginning.

We can make decisions, begin practices and start habits *now* that will reap a harvest of goodness and life in our hearts and in those around us.

We can decide that *this is the time* to chart a new course, and to take on a new identity in these things, leaving the past behind.

If we so choose, self-nurture will not only imprint our souls with a fresh perspective, but over time and as we pursue new behaviours, will embed lasting change and perpetual development.

It is a tremendous source of life and power, and as we dig searchingly away at the previously parched ground, offers up a fountain of life and truth.

Time

One of the first and most crucial elements we must address if we are to self-nurture effectively is the management of our time. Time is one of our most precious commodities.

Time is life, and time is wealth.

And time is health.

Perhaps most importantly, we can be absolutely certain that our time in life is limited and finite, a wonderful theme inherent to humanity.

One day, on a gravestone somewhere, on an order of service, there will be our name and then two numbers with a gap of years between them.

That gap will contain the time given to us on this earth.

Those few years are the time that we have. It is a distance that diminishes daily, hourly, moment by moment and without ceasing.

One day like a clock stopping quietly on a distant mantelpiece, the gentle rhythm within us will slow and cease, and our time will be gone forever.

We would do well to be brave enough to accept that within the confines of such certain fragility, taking responsibility for and diligently managing our time is incredibly important.

This is a truth that I think is surely universally momentous for us all, whatever our circumstances or our identity.

Nevertheless, where we are immensely different is in the staggering diversity of our individual lives and situations.

With this knowledge, I must recognise the futility of attempting to offer simplistic rules or guidelines for any pattern of self-nurture in regard to one or another individual's time.

Instead, I hope I may simply suggest and look at some basic principles that may help us to spend our time wisely and in the pursuit of that which will incrementally heal us, bear fruit and help us along the rocky path towards true awareness.

Aloneness and Reflection

All humans are frightened of their own solitude.
Yet only in solitude can man learn to know himself.

Han Suyin, from *The Mountain is Young*

One of the things that defines aware people and those that develop and sustain an ongoing healthy self-nurture is their ability to find and then utilise times of regular aloneness for personal reflection in which they create quiet space around themselves and remove themselves from the routine and volume of life in order to focus on their inner-self.

Before I elaborate, it is important to say that I don't mean to imply that such people wallow in loneliness. Loneliness is an incredibly powerful and destructive phenomenon, suffered by the many millions in our generation experiencing the vast debilitating emptiness brought about by an ongoing disconnectedness from those around them.

Loneliness is never chosen, it can only ever be suffered and endured.

It is an entirely unwelcome affliction that eats away at the soul like a quiet ravaging cancer.

If unchecked, it will hollow out a human life until it is a dry shell.

Perhaps more than our orientation towards anything else, our humanity is meant to be regularly relational, connected, communal, and interdependent and the sustained removal of an individual from this life-giving rhythm can only ever be catastrophic.

Of all our many widespread psychological, emotional, spiritual and physical illnesses, loneliness looms in our modern 'civilised' society as the most endemic, the most widespread and certainly in my view the most damaging to humankind.

Despite our widespread collective cultural oblivion, its great dark shadow towers over our modern world. In fact if we look carefully, our society today is more than at any other time in human history structured to facilitate and to inculcate individual loneliness because in the modern world, society's fiscal success and survival partially depends on it. Much of our financial system and capitalist model relies entirely upon people being alone; unfulfilled and spiritually hungry so that they can be relentlessly told by ravenous advertisers that they need something *else*; something *new* in their lives and that through its purchase they can finally *buy* that elusive sense of happiness and peace.

Furthermore – despite operating under the ludicrous trumpeting banner of 'connection' – the internet may have done more than anything else in human history to isolate many millions of individuals and permanently confine their psyches and hearts to communicate and function via a keyboard and 2-dimensional screen through which they can visit and enjoy each and every conceivable type of human phenomenon or desire as a voyeur, except the true human interaction and genuine intimacy that one requires to truly inhabit his or her humanity and achieve fruitfulness and growth.

Loneliness slowly strips us of our identity, our voice, our heart, our love.

It is an incredibly serious and powerful sickness that afflicts so very many.

Futhermore, part of the reason that loneliness is so toxic is that despite their possible oblivion, it invariably renders its subjects forgotten, voiceless, and abandoned to a silent fate. Many millions in our world stand quietly and hopefully waiting at a door that may never be opened to them.

No-one hears the lonely cry out because their voice only echoes in the place of their own isolation and solitude.

Even so, despite what we might presume, many of the most severe cases of human loneliness are found in individuals who are actually married, often parents themselves and integrated within families – in fact people who may appear to be relationally or by societal standards, successfully surrounded by others.

Truthfully, however, in a very real sense they are utterly and completely isolated from anyone and confined to a deep inner loneliness.

I have known so very many such isolated people, who although appearing daily to function in the perceived normality of lasting familial relationships to those outside, suffer regularly from an aching loneliness that is never vanquished. Tragically, they are often aware enough to recognise (a brutally painful realisation) that they still largely live out their busy lives in a profoundly isolated world.

But simultaneously, few of us are able to address such reality constructively and hence overcome it in any real or lasting way, because we simply don't know how and are afraid to face such knowledge.

In contrast to the terrible affliction of human loneliness, an individual's prioritisation of periods of chosen aloneness require us to carefully carve out times of solitude for ourselves in which we can simply be alone; meditate, rest and most importantly of all *reflect* upon our lives, our relationships, our journeys and our souls.

Such periods are so very precious in our human existence, but they can only be fruitful if they are prioritised and protected as regular time in which we are not chained to our smartphones, watching TV, listening to music or all those other countless modern distractions.

Despite having importance and value in our lives, if unregulated, such habits tend to isolate and somehow disconnect us from true thought and simply 'being'; inhabiting our own humanity in the quietness of our existence and exploring our true thoughts and feelings.

One of the very interesting phenomena I have witnessed in many of those most damaged and ravaged by abuse and darkness, is their abject terror of aloneness – their complete inability to be in any way secure and comfortable in the spacious quiet of solitude.

I have known many clients who would literally rather cut and even kill themselves than spend a few hours alone and face the resulting reality of the thought life that so tortures them.

One of the signs of the painstaking eventual healing in such individuals is often manifested as they courageously begin to tentatively spend just a few moments and then increasingly longer, quietly and comfortably alone, finally discovering a hard fought inner safety and rest, as they begin to rebuild their shattered inner psychological landscape.

I wonder if such issues are simply exacerbated in our modern world of relentless bombardment by texts, statuses, tweets, headlines, adverts, score lines, newsflashes – brought to us 24 hours a day via our ever present accumulation of smartphones and laptops.

I realised recently that despite being a relative technophobe I now possess an iPhone and 2 MacBooks plus another personal laptop, a work Blackberry and FlyBook for my job, another work PC, and another additional phone in order to conduct my daily life and communicate!?

On some days I might receive between 20 and 30 personal texts requiring response, 20 or so personal emails, 40 to 50 work emails and anything between 10 and 20 work calls, many of them quite urgent.

Invariably, from the moment I wake to the moment I sleep, my daily thoughts, actions and feelings are profoundly affected by the constant barrage of communications on a dizzying array of devices on which I can also check news headlines, watch films and TV and access the relentless barrage of social networking resources.

I know that I am certainly not alone in this regard.

What are so many millions of us doing in the name of mistakenly assumed 'connection' to our fragile psyches, imaginations and thought lives by living in such a peculiar way, for the first time in our human history?

What might happen if each of us turned all these devices off for a few moments or hours per day and quietly thought to ourselves and simply reflected?

The ability to inculcate and develop a vibrant and healthy ongoing capacity for self-reflection is perhaps the most valuable gift we can impart to our fellow searchers after healing and truth because therein lies the necessary and elusive power to birth the fledgling foundations of inner change.

And in ourselves, the ability to reflect wisely and patiently is the most important element of all within self-nurture and must make up the foundation of all of our time spent alone.

If we create and utilise such times wisely in what is true reflection, no other resource can enable us with so much helpful scope in which to identify opportunity for change, progress and crucial self-encouragement.

Time in which to learn to think, and to learn to grow.

Time alone is such a wonderful opportunity but no-one can be overly prescriptive about the way in which we spend it, other than to suggest that we patiently seek that which affords us inner reflection in a safe and quiet context.

Some of us require an hour or more a few times a week in quiet to piece together our thoughts and emotions and make useful sense of them to think things over.

For others of us, a few minutes at the start or end of each day, the commute to work or drive back from school after dropping the kids is the only time we may have in which to reflect and self-nurture.

Nevertheless, whatever the duration, place or method, we would do well to consider that time alone spent simply *thinking* about ourselves and our lives is a glorious gift, if only we can employ our mind and our thoughts as willing servants rather than a bullying master.

Such thinking is so terribly important to us; our thoughts and their nature inform the root of everything within our souls and minds.

If our minds are enemies to us through negativity, anxiety, anger or fear, we can become held hostage in our own lives; confined in a kind of numb paralysis defined by a terrible inner powerlessness and victimhood. If this is the case, how can we change?

How can we find a way to approach thinking healthily in order to take back control and maximise optimum healing and progress on the steep journey through our complicated and difficult lives?

Many of the people I have worked with suffer under such great affliction as a direct result of the fact that they have a deeply unhealthy thought life and are unable to stem the chaotic upset that ensues.

For out of our thoughts, made manifest is the power for good or for ill in our lives and relationships.

Despite our best attempts at avoiding and diverting the consequences of such truth, this reality cannot be overturned.

Once again, such themes are immensely complicated and too momentous to explain away simplistically.

But let us try to consider that once again we are simply explorers of these great mysteries and we can only proceed with humility and accept our great need for guidance and change.

For now, let us think a little more about what constitutes the regular practise of wise and healthy reflection.

We have talked much about the nature of life and the many seasons of challenge that we must face on this great journey.

One of the things we might find helpful in terms of understanding ourselves as we navigate the ever changing landscapes of our uncertain lives with a view to development, is *to find a consistent way of recording what it is we actually think and feel about ourselves and about experiences in our lives.*

This practice is absolutely essential to facilitate and empower true change as we pass through the many hundreds of stages that we must traverse as we continue on our winding path.

Recording is a terribly important part of the crucial *cumulative* process of self-reflection, because in our humanity, many of us tend to be orientated towards two things that significantly undermine and beset progress; forgetfulness and self-deception.

It is amazing how quickly we can forget that which is crucial to remember in order for us to learn.

It is staggering how as humans we can manipulate and disfigure memory and true perspective in order to avoid the tiresome work of facing the necessity of crucial change, exposed by us seeing things as they really, truthfully are.

We must learn to love such truth.

To honour and to revere it.

To record it.

And then in sustained practise to take responsibility for its increased unearthing.

In order to do so, we must bravely face certain unpalatable reminders.

Like water running down rock, our humanity predicates our tendency to always seek the path of least resistance in life.

We are orientated towards comfort and ease.

We are often lazy.

We can be astoundingly arrogant and wholly oblivious to our great ignorance.

In our inner nature, there is a deep part of us that hates change and longs to be constantly told that it is perfectly acceptable for us to be left alone and to remain the same.

Fundamental change of ourselves within, so very often terrifies us.

It is for this reason that as previously said, so many individuals only find truth and revelation through the brokenness of tragedy and intense personal suffering; because such experience tends to strip away the immensely powerful structures of incumbent ego that restrict our view of things as they really are, in order to perpetuate a paradigm in which we are *always* right.

Many of us tend to process the inevitable daily challenges to such deluded certainty, as outrageous attacks on our person — in which we inevitably become incandescent victims.

But the simple truth is deafening and echoes throughout all of human consciousness whether we will listen and enjoy the tremendous inherent blessings, or flee and be consigned to what feels comfortable but is actually cowardice and stagnation.

In every season of our brief lives here on this beautiful planet, we all need change of mind like we need oxygen.

We are *all* in regular need of events, experiences and challenging people through which is revealed; *transformative truth that will enlighten us*.

It is in the acceptance and assimilation of such ongoing revelation that we might learn to finally challenge and break down the false paradigms within, that so restrict our growth.

Reflective recording in ongoing discipline is an enormous part of this process and we must embrace it.

Reflective Discipline

*I write because I don't know what I think
until I read what I say.*

Flannery O' Connor

To close the first part of this book, I want to suggest a simple and accessible model for the practice of reflective recording that I hope might encourage its undertaking in a practical and real way that impacts our lives.

If prioritised and diligently pursued in sincerity, this discipline will be the fundamental driver in building and growing a cumulative wisdom and deep awareness.

The primary goal of individual reflectiveness and the most crucial part of this awareness is the ability to foster and then develop an *objective view* or perspective within one's own psyche, from which we can draw and then reflect upon previously hidden conclusions.

And it is the lack of such a wise and living objectivity within personal thought and action that is the primary cause of all mental, psychological and relational illness.

Without any mechanism of objectivity within our own minds, we are simply confined to react to everything that we feel and think – regardless of whether it is wise and healthy for us to do so.

Objective thought is all that restrains us from doing so, to our great benefit, blessing, and service.

Our conscience only works as an objective mechanism, as does our ability to understand and empathise with others and our ability to consider consequences. Without such crucial faculties being developed and nurtured, our psyches are precariously unbalanced and vulnerable to real danger.

In extreme cases, in the moment and seemingly without second thought, we can make staggeringly destructive decisions that have lifelong repercussions for ourselves and for others.

I recently watched a documentary about death row in Texas in which many of the prisoners awaiting this ultimate penalty appeared so very young compared to me in my mid-thirties.

As I watched face after face during interview, often disfigured with guilt, anguish and torment at the gravity of their actions and their consequential fate, I wondered how it is possible that these lives and those of their victims are so destroyed by acts unspeakable.

And for what?

As a consequence, years in prison and a torturous wait for a young mind and heart that will soon be likely snuffed out by the bloodthirsty revenge of societal 'justice'.

As the stories of these young lives were relayed one by one and details explained, it suddenly struck me thunderously, that what many of them lacked in that life-changing moment of testing and great need immediately before their often opportunistic crimes unfolded, was the presence of something *within* preventing them: an inner voice imploring them to run and to flee, to think of their victims and the consequences of their actions.

Without such a voice, how many of us could avoid a similar fate given circumstances of extreme duress, blind anger, intense peer pressure and most commonly, the existence of deep emotional poverty and prior suffering transfixed in a crucible of loneliness?

The ability to transcend our immediate emotional situational responses and to reflect carefully back upon ourselves in order to make objective judgments, is imperative to our existence if we are to live safely, wisely and fruitfully amongst our fellow humans.

It is a skill a little like a muscle – it can and will grow, but it must be isolated and then trained in order to develop to its best and healthiest potential. And this is where I must return to the practice of regular reflection and recording on specific issues becoming so very useful.

I recognise of course, that many of us are well acquainted with and regularly practise techniques of very effective self-nurture in our times alone.

Others of us keep regular diaries and journals on our life journey and read back regularly, providing a wonderful tool for the principles I am discussing.

But others of us may find help in simple patterns and the learnt techniques I want to describe so simply.

To this end, I hope to be able to suggest a technique that if unconsidered before, might help us experiment in order to begin our navigation of the reflective process within our own thoughts.

However, it is important to say that, rather than becoming a habit or an end in itself, I hope that it will simply facilitate an objective way of thinking that develops continuously until we have no need of following such patterns and find that we are thinking and reflecting objectively and with integrity 'unconsciously'.

As we draw to a close on this first part of our journey, if you are willing to learn to reflect – to nurture and develop this skill within, the next time you have time alone and can be quiet for a few minutes, use a pen and a bit of paper or your mobile or laptop, and write down a theme or personal situation that you are currently facing in your life that you might like to focus upon in order to see change or progress.

The second part of this book is a collection of chapters that I hope may provide a little stimulation and provide some practice in using it.

Think deeply for a moment and quiet your mind. Choose an area in which you would like to gain greater wisdom, an issue that you are facing, or something in which you would like to grow.

You might want to find somewhere that is particularly calming for you personally – for me I walk or sit beside the quiet sea opposite my flat.

I find that alone in nature and particularly in the presence of the sea, I can feel and sense and hear in a way that proves impossible around people or buildings or traffic. I have been this way about the sea since I was a little boy, wherever I have travelled or lived in the world. It is my sacred place. There I find the path that leads to my soul.

I believe that nature is actually for all of us the sacred place in which we can draw the most truth, the most beauty, the most revelation – if only we prioritise quiet time there.

When you have found your place for reflection, write down in your own words:

What has happened or what happens; what is the <u>reality</u> of your current situation on the theme or issue that you want to focus on?

Secondly: Take your time. Think deeply. Then, write down how this reality or issue makes you <u>feel</u>. How does it affect you?

Thirdly: Think deeply and patiently. Is there anything you might be learning or could <u>learn</u> from this situation?

Finally, take time to wonder, meditate and think deeply:

What could you change or do <u>differently</u> and how might that look?

Take time to think patiently while you answer these questions.

Jot down as much about the thoughts and feeling that emerge as you can.

It goes without saying that we must be careful to record in a place that is confidential, because it is absolutely crucial that we write nakedly, honestly and that where possible we focus on the challenging and complex aspects of our life and relationships.

But I cannot stress enough how the most important element of this practice is our willingness to *prioritise* such quiet thinking and writing time, to complete it and then to continue with regularity, *making certain that we always read back our previous attempts and thoughts.*

It is only the discipline of doing so *repeatedly* that holds the power to bring real and lasting change within.

At times, and initially in the beginning, we may find the process frustrating, clumsy, and awkward.

But if only we can quietly and determinedly persist, *we will find that it gently begins to coax forth and reveal a slowly developing awareness — the emergence of an objective understanding of which we may have been previously unaware but that will become central to our responses and to the way that we feel.*

We will discover, and then grow in, the wisdom that lies within each of us. Just as Jane Austen explains: '*we have all a better guide in ourselves, if we would attend to it, than any other person can be.*'

This reflective discipline will begin to change our heart from within.

As we truly persist, we will find ourselves becoming reflective and thoughtful people.

We will be inspired to find deeper answers to questions and challenges that emerge from a quiet place inside ourselves.

We will learn such a tremendous amount about ourselves and about the way that we actually are in our own thoughts and feelings, if only we are willing to look deeply.

We may notice traits and ways of looking at things that we deplore in ourself and will want to change, and also things of which we can be truly proud and can develop and celebrate.

But we will learn.

Such reflection is a great beginning for us.

If only we will consider and pursue it, we will surely find that it is the foundation and source of life-changing power.

And through it, we will begin to grow in an objective and nurturing relationship within ourselves that will propel change.

★★★

I want to end the first section of this book with the acknowledgement that the 4 step process I have described and its discipline that I am suggesting, may appear insignificant and even simplistic on first view.

To encourage us to consider and to experiment, I want to close by relaying a wonderful ancient story from many millennia past that contains a great truth about the achievement of true healing and humility.

Many thousands of generations ago, in the days of the great Syrian eastern empire, there was a man called Namaan.

He was a fearsome military commander amongst his people, feted for his success on the battlefield. But for all of his great fame and wealth, Namaan was stricken with incurable leprosy, a terrible affliction in those days.

The story is told that through a young girl serving in his household, Namaan heard tell of a Holy man with great power, who could heal. Desperate to be made whole, he willingly journeyed to seek a miracle.

But to his outrage, when he finally arrived, the healing Prophet would not even come out to speak with Namaan and instead, sent his servant to communicate on his behalf, bearing the message that if he were to wash in the River Jordan seven times that he would be healed.

Angry, disappointed and insulted, Namaan turned back to start his long journey home.

The story might have ended like this, and his fate be ultimately sealed, but Namaan had wisdom with him.

You too have this wisdom within: your *conscience*; – your 'knowledge within.'

One of his servants bravely challenged him, gently imploring him to consider that if he had been required by the Prophet to fulfil a *great* task, that he would have gladly done it.

How much simpler then, to simply wash in the river?

And Namaan listened to his servant, and went down and washed.

And he was made completely whole.

I love this ancient story because it contains such profound and visceral truth about our humanity and the way in which we regularly set fixed and certain pre-conditions for our own healing and redemption.

Often, if revelation and light come to us outside of our own preconditions, expectations or from beyond our cherished understanding, however simple the implications for us to respond and to consider change, we simply reject them because they do not conform to our view of how we can and should grow.

Our pride and certainty so easily obscure and remove the possibility of true and lasting healing for us.

But the truth is that: we can be utterly changed and transformed *today*.

We need only humbly see that our healing lies within our acceptance of true humility, and then our willingness to step out of the confines of what we know.

To embrace mystery and faith in the unknown – the willingness to experiment and venture outwards from our safe place of our relentless personal certainty, pride and identity.

If we truly seek change, it may just be time to be willing and brave.

To finally trust and then step out in something new.

For if we want something we have never had before, we must be willing to do something we have never done before.

This is Awareness.

This is Wisdom.

This is Life.

Relationships
& Fruitfulness

The world we have created is a process of our thinking.
It cannot be changed without changing our thinking.

Albert Einstein

In the second part of this book, I want to provide some individual chapters that expand upon the previous themes but that are designed to be read in relation to you as a person about your own inner journey.

They can be easily used alongside the reflective model in the last chapter.

In this way I hope that what follows will be both a thematic and a practical introduction to individual reflection and that this wonderful gift and ability that lies within each of us, will become a profound blessing to you and a discipline that ultimately becomes the cornerstone of life.

What for you is
Non-Negotiable?

One of the questions I ask clients to think about in the Retreat work that I direct is:

'What for you is Non-Negotiable?'

In the introductory session of the retreat, I encourage delegates to think honestly and carefully as individuals about what might be the essential practices or elements in their life, work and relationships without which they would be unable to function or exist.

It is an endlessly interesting exercise because, of the many people from a whole range of backgrounds with whom I have worked, all without exception have to think intently for some time before journalling their answers.

Furthermore, when as a group we discuss how it may have felt thinking in this way, delegates invariably confess that they have barely ever thought such a question through for themselves, or ever considered its implications for life and personal growth.

Often those keen to share their answers describe the most fascinating essentials on which psychological wellbeing rests and without which they would struggle to cope.

Naturally there are many who are certain that time and closeness to their children or partners are the only thing that they couldn't negotiate on, but others seem committed to agonising over this question — even if what is uncovered is uncomfortable — in an attempt to greater understand themselves and pursue personal change and growth.

One successful businessman shared quietly that after thinking intently for nearly five minutes, he ultimately challenged himself to write completely honestly and wrote about his addiction to the gym and his countless hours spent there, often to the detriment of his family life and the cause of much conflict in his marriage.

Another delegate tentatively shared that without her hour of yoga and meditation every morning, she knew without any doubt that her marriage would quickly crumble as would her psychological health and her ability to do her job as a Senior Leader.

I have been privileged to hear people both relay and grapple with the most remarkable and unexpected things when they really consider such a question deeply, bravely, honestly and with a view to exploring themselves and unearthing that which is hidden in their lives.

Often, when we are courageous with ourselves and are willing to look a little deeper into such questions, there is a wealth of truth and revelation waiting to be discovered that can lead to personal challenge, renewal and subsequent inspiration.

I ask my clients to consider 10 different personal 'Life' questions on the Awareness/Change days that I direct. All 10 are about individual values, thoughts, backgrounds, influences, relationships, hopes and personal ambitions.

I have never yet had a single delegate either prepared with an answer or respond that they have ever thought about any of the questions raised.

I find this phenomenon endlessly fascinating.

Many of us seem to live a life that in the words of John Lennon, actually happens when we are 'busy making other plans'. We often live carried along by the force of external events or by our unexamined actions, habits and choices, despite the fact that they have significant and far-reaching consequences.

We tend to spend little time reflecting on the deep questions, missing the fact that the answers to these questions actually underpin all that we do and feel, every moment, every hour, every day.

In the overwhelming information bombardment of our modern 'connected' world, it occurs to me that in our constant busyness and the relentless challenge of balancing the multiple demands on us, we may be missing the element that in our humanity is most essential to our growth and wellbeing; personal time in which to reflect and challenge ourselves with a view to change.

The willingness and discipline to take time out to think about what we really feel and think and the values that underpin our actions and behaviours holds enormous power to bring healing, positive change and true growth.

We might do well to prioritise it.

Reflect:

What for YOU is non-negotiable?

What have been the consequences in your life?

Are these good things, or bad?

How might you either prioritise them more, or overcome them?

The Cost of Exposure

In watching a recent documentary about Whitney Houston's shocking descent into drug abuse and mental illness and her tragic premature death, it struck me again just how many profoundly gifted people who become famous become unable to cope with the weight and consequences of their own success.

I think of so many heroes of mine – amazing musicians, sportsmen and actors – who have reached the heights of fame and fortune, only to succumb to addiction and excess and ultimately, to lose their lives because of it.

In fact it might be true to say that this is the norm, and not the exception amongst successful and famous people throughout the ages.

I have written, wondered and thought much about the reasons for this, and until recently, I always thought that this phenomenon was caused by the heightened availability of such substances and industry standard excesses in which the powerful and successful lived out their privileged lives or the stresses of fame.

But I don't believe this anymore.

I now believe that the reason that so many famous people become dependent on drugs and alcohol to cope, is because their fame means that they find a large part of themselves utterly *exposed* on a daily basis to the world around them with no protective boundaries.

Not only do they now comprise the present person that is within them – that they have grown up with and become accustomed to residing within their body – but they have another identity that is constantly and relentlessly being dissected and pored over and ravaged by incalculable external forces.

They can no more control this part of themselves and its fate, than they can control the weather.

But it still feels like a deep part of them, and they may have poured their heart into this identity... but it is no longer under their jurisdiction or control.

The daily knowledge of such relentless un-boundaried exposure of a large part of oneself to the world, is staggeringly unhealthy for a human soul.

And the resulting agony and discomfort is only bearable if one can anaesthetise oneself to the constant knowledge of such acute exposure.

As I have thought about this, I have seen that the exposure of oneself, one's image and one's identity to the constant scrutiny of outside judgment and opinion and response, invariably leads to mental illness and self-destruction in humans.

Such exposure is likely – despite its seductive initial excitement and titillation – to ultimately curse and ravage the fragile psyche and sensitive identity of a human soul.

And yet, in our modern 'connected' culture, many of our children and young people are already well embarked on this fateful journey.

Their identity is increasingly one that is online, that is available to the outside world and constantly present, with no boundaries or protection.

It is no wonder that our current generation is being revealed to be the most medicated, depressed, suicidal, anxious and unhappy in all of human history.

Because we have allowed a world in which our children have an online identity and image that is constantly exposed, and an ever present and all-consuming concern to them.

When this is going well for them, they become addicted to the dopamine surge of 'like' fuelled acceptance.

When it goes badly, I fear that the fragile and still developing mental health of our young people, will be scarred beyond all recognition.

In years to come I believe that we may see the true cost of a dynamic that we have happily accepted; to their wellness and mental health.

I hope that I am wrong.

Reflect:

Have you ever felt exposed by Social Media?

What have been the consequences in your life?

How often do you spend time away from all devices?

The Question We Never Dare Ask Our Children

Over many years I have regularly had the opportunity to work with parents as they struggle to nurture and develop their precious and yet challenging children.

I am a father myself, and even as an amateur (having co-parented only one child) I consider the job of parenting to be by far the most difficult and certainly among the most important that we face in our lifetime.

There are many reasons for this view, but perhaps the most significant is that if we choose to commit to parenting with all of our hearts, then we find that the inherent suffering, joy and sheer gravity *exposes* us more than anything else that we can experience in human life.

To a great extent, we can and do hide from ourselves and from others in so many other human relationships. But our children expose us as we truly are - and this is both a wonderful and a frightening thing. Despite all of our expertise, idealism and certainty as new parents, we are often unaware of this particular phenomenon before the journey begins and it is invariably a tremendous shock to our psyche and ego when we notice our true selves, often for the first time, being painfully revealed.

And yet parenthood is so infinitely valuable to humanity primarily because of this exposure: Because humans would by no means expose themselves to such complete vulnerability and truth unless they were forced to by the regularly implacable nature of the love that they find in their hearts for their difficult offspring, binding them irrevocably to life's most ingenious breaking process.

It is no surprise that such a large number of people flee the responsibility of intimate child rearing at the first opportunity, or as in so very many generations past and still today, close themselves off from the agony and tension of wholehearted engagement; distancing themselves. Speedily, many simply let their partner bear the weight alone, citing all kinds of rational reasons to themselves and anyone who will listen or ask. Tragically, as is so overwhelmingly common in my individualistic generation, many abandon the struggle entirely as the story of their child's life unfolds.

I have seen such a diverse range of parental journeys and witnessed such agony and such beauty. I have worked 1:1 in crisis intervention with those who have been the victims of staggeringly abusive and dysfunctional parenting dynamics; with children who have no memory of a life without endless days of pain at the hands of the adults meant to protect and to care for them.

I have also worked with parents who have made me feel utterly inadequate and then deeply envious as I have witnessed their seemingly effortless parental gifts and abilities.

As years have passed, several things have struck me about the challenge of parenting that I think the perpetual busyness of modern life causes us to miss.

The first is that with hardly any human exception, all of us want to be good parents to our children, and invariably we think that we are just that.

It is rare to find a parent who in the process of their striving, doesn't consider themselves to be a good or a worthy parent.

I have even worked with individuals who are utterly convinced of such ability, simultaneous to attempting to explain away the shocking harm that they have inflicted upon their young.

Some of us hear such things and shudder, wondering how such human blindness can exist.

And yet, this is not the greatest blindness that I have seen in parents.

The greatest blindness I have seen is in me, and in the overwhelming majority of parents that I have worked with and known.

This blindness is not an evil or an abuse, it is just a profound kind of oblivion:

As human parents we love our children deeply and often believe ourselves to be good parents.

From the very beginnings of new life, we launch ourselves into our task with well-intended fervour, commitment and certainty.

But not once, at any single time during our children's up-bringing, do we ever once ask them *what we are like as parents*.

Not once.

Peculiarly, we are not aware or brave enough in western culture to make our children stakeholders in their own childhood.

It would be too great a risk, too real for us. It would make us too accountable and this frightens us more than anything.

Instead, we are more than satisfied to simply assume on their behalf, year after year after year.

In our complacency, we are so certain that we are a particular person — the cleverly manufactured one in our own mind and of our own making — that we easily convince ourselves that our children simply know us to be and see us as this individual.

This is a profound blindness.

Because our children can see. They often see much more deeply than we do.

They can see from an incredibly young age, who we really are. I have seen the evidence for such intuition and discernment in children in more situations than I can count.

We should bravely and humbly build an ongoing dialogue with them as soon as they can talk; about who we really are as people.

We should give them a voice in the relational dynamic that will affect them most on the rocky and wonderful adventure that is their painful, beautiful lives.

Gently, peacefully, exploratively, we should take the time and invest the courage that it takes to build that most crucial of all dialogues and ask them repeatedly, creatively, respectfully:

... what am I like as a father or mother?

And then we should listen.

Reflect:

Have you ever had these types of conversations with your children or your parents?

What have been the consequences?

Has the outcome been good or bad for your relationship?

How might you prioritise such conversations more?

The Gap That Exists Within Me

One of the things that has struck me over many years of working through the exploration of my own soul and in my co-work with other individuals around their inner struggles and life challenges, is the *gap* that exists in each and every one of us.

The gap between who we project that we are to others – our families, those we work with, the outside world – and the other person that *we* live with and know that is truly us.

All of us live with the knowledge of this gap to a lesser or greater extent, depending on our self-awareness and integrity.

We may lie and pretend that there is no gap, but we are only deceiving ourselves... and somewhere within we know it.

For some of us, the pain of such knowledge is too great and we looked away many years ago and have lived a life since of self-deception and suppression – pretending that the gap does not exist and that we are whole, acceptable to ourselves, fully sorted and absolutely OK.

But for others of us, day by day, the gap has become familiar to us, we are aware of it – it quietly haunts us as we make our way through life and attempt to find peace, while it casts its thrumming shadow over us, ever louder, ever closer, an echo of true self-knowledge deep within our soul.

The width of the gap with which we live, dictates how hard we must search for wholeness and the peace that we may be able or may fail to find.

The true pursuit of our lives, of our humanity, of our complex soul, must be to face the reality of the gap and to perhaps someday, somehow resolve it.

Many of us find ourselves spurred on by the dream that one day we will be able to live as one – a complete person who is the same within as without, the same person alone as with others, one in whom there is no gap, no pretence.

As I have thought and wondered about this phenomenon I have begun to think about the other gaps that we experience and struggle with in our humanity. The gaps that regularly haunt us and must be fought and wrestled with.

Much of human anxiety is caused by a gap: between how we *sense* and *wish* that things could be for us in our lives and situation... and how such things truly are.

The width of the gap between these two perceptions will be the extent of our anxiety and often represents the scale of our battle to overcome it.

The gap that causes us to be depressed; between how we want our world and our situation to be, and how we know or feel that it really is. The width of this gap will often be the magnitude of our depression and the measure of our struggle with it.

As I have agonised over these things, I have realised that there is a deep and profound reason for these gaps, a root that binds us inextricably to our humanity and that separates us from all other life that exists on earth.

It is that each and every one of us has the deep sense within that in ourselves as individuals, and in our lives, that things should be a particular way.

That things should be different to how they are and how we experience them and know them to be.

We cannot accept ourselves as we discover what we truly are.

We cannot accept our fate.

Somewhere within our deepest nature, we strive; we pace the room buried deep within our hearts and souls, and dream and sigh and wait for something that we are aware that we do not have.

We *long*.

We are filled with longing and then a peculiar kind of grief and disappointment as life and ourselves are gradually revealed to us as they actually are... and there revealed: is the gap.

On a psychological level, there are several responses to the gap and to our inner sense of its presence within. We can attempt to lose ourselves in a career, material wealth, the pursuit of success, the drug of romance, the fantasy of popularity, the anaesthetic of security.

We learn to push and expand the false and 'well' identity that we have built within ourselves to try to cover the gap by learning to overplay our abilities and achievements – to inflate our sense of 'self' and the 'enough-ness' of us in an attempt to quiet the sense of gap.

Everything within our wildly individualistic and materialistic culture has been built upon humanity's need for this self-expansion and ensures that there are always a myriad of distractions to our inner malaise by constantly drowning us in information, possessions, entertainment and titillation.

Alternatively, and when we don't choose this path, our quiet inner sense of the gap leads us to nurse a creeping guilt, shame even, and ultimately results in anxiety and insecurity about who we really are.

Fascinatingly, a staggering amount of anxiety and depression has at its root the fear of being *exposed*; the terror of life itself revealing us to be rotten and shameful.

Such anxiety is magnified because we are so self-obsessed and inward-looking as a result of our uncomfortableness, that we fail to understand that so very many others share just the same fear and simply cover it well.

But the problem with these deeply human responses, is that none of them are *real*.

None really face the questions and challenges that must be stared down – none are truly satisfying because none truly resonate within us as truthful.

Instead, what I have seen as I have looked at life in this way, is a profound and staggering truth:

More than anything else, the gap makes us as human people and as a race, *vulnerable*.

Because we are not whole, and we know it, we are vulnerable because we long, we *need* to quiet the sound of the gap with answers that we feel that we understand and that fit.

And in desperately searching for satisfying answers from such vulnerability, we become blinded and then addicted to the terrible folly *of our own certainty*.

Certainty is the thing that humanity has created for itself in order to counter and silence and paper over the gap in order to drown it out – to bury it once and for all.

Our profound addiction to 'certainty' and the possessing of absolute truth is the most human thing about us, whether it be manifested through our self-made gods of religion, ideology, politics, science or individualism.

We are certain of something or other and then we believe that we are right because of what we think – we are sure that we know 'the truth.'

And we genuinely believe that our so-called 'possession' of such truth destroys the gap once and for all, saving us from what seems like our insecure fate in the wildness of the vast universe.

The lure of being right and possessing the 'truth' for ourselves, is the intoxicating and irresistible drug that we use as a race, that we have always used, to slake our thirst for wholeness.

I have never known, nor seen, nor heard or ever met a human who is not like me and addicted to his or her pursuit of and belief in this individual absolutism; from birth until death.

And this is why humanity and her pursuit of certainty and rightness serve as such a tragic and divisive storyline throughout the entire history of our beautiful infant race.

Because it is *this pride and its ability to exploit our vulnerability* that has rendered us so profoundly fragmented, broken, lost and wrong and more cursed than we will ever truly know, imprisoning us in our sense of self-rightness and distancing us irrevocably from our brothers and sisters who are just like us – who bear the same gap, the same wound that might unite us.

This can never be mentioned or faced – the consequences are too great, the alternative too terrifying.

Because the alternative is finally *facing and owning the gap and accepting it as part of me*.

The alternative is turning from answers and rightness and our imagined possession of absolute truth, and turning from the search for security... and instead embracing mystery and humility and wonder.

The alternative is facing the true predicament of my being, and then in childlike faith, accepting it and trusting.

I see a strange thing today as I watch a nature documentary on TV.

An antelope, stalked by a beautiful lioness, is finally overcome and as she struggles to fight the overwhelming power and strength of her attacker and is finally conquered, I see something profound and heart-stopping happen in her movement, in her eyes, in her story.

There is finally a point at which she can fight no more, she is utterly overcome, her end is nigh and then I see something that causes me to catch my breath as I stare in rapt wonder and awe.

She looks up, and in her face is pure Acceptance.

She will die now and her breathing, hearing and seeing is over.

But she has fought and lost and can now utterly accept that which has swept over her. She is full of peace and I see it in her, crystal clear and magnificent.

Moments later she is gone. Life extinguished and her blood flows.

But she died in the knowledge and peace of something that is far beyond my striving, conflicted race:

acceptance and that which is its fruit:

Peace.

Reflect:

Do you recognise the sense of Gap in yourself?

What have been the consequences in your life?

Are these good things, or bad?

How might you accept the Gap and find peace?

The Failure of Success

Modern culture becomes ever more obsessed with the pursuit and worship of human success.

Our numerous and ever present social media inlets convey a perpetual drip-feed of success-porn, trumpeting the expertise, wealth, beauty, lifestyle or career of any person, product or service that will guarantee us victory in whatever area we are assured that the subject has 'conquered' life.

Our lonely postmodern generation quietly struggles in a great cauldron of covetousness – we seem peculiarly exploitable and vulnerable due to our creeping insecurity; increasingly disillusioned by the political, philosophical and societal aspirations behind which we hid in previous generations.

Religion and ideology have failed us, because they are based around man and man eventually corrupts all that he touches.

And now, in the 21st century, we pursue all that we have left: ourselves.

Consequently, our culture struggles under a tide of individualism that tells its anxious young people that the success of their own desires and dreams is the only answer in life; and if only they believe and follow shall they become great and achieve what they are assured will be 'happiness'.

Such a gospel may prove to be more perilous to the future of the planet and to humankind than any that has ever existed in our chaotic history; but society has turned in upon itself and like so many extinct civilisations and creatures that have gone before, we face ultimate spiritual starvation as we feed upon ourselves.

Nevertheless; the uncomfortable truth about profit remains – Telling people that they deserve and need success and that it is within their grasp, will sell almost anything to a fragile young person.

Such a phenomenon exists not least because our psyches are profoundly vulnerable to the daily insecurity that we are not and do not possess enough.

Coupled with our overwhelming social media driven narcissism and longing towards future glory; and this is a heady mix.

Just tell us that such glory can be achieved through our own efforts combined with a 'magic' formula, taught or given to us by a person or a belief-system in whom we can indulge our human urge to follow, and to worship.

Or simply inform a fragile and developing individual that you can show them how to solve all of their problems, make millions of pounds, gain the perfect physique, achieve the perfect career, find the perfect partner, or achieve their dreams.

Package it right, and they will follow you to the ends of the earth and pay you for the privilege, as long as you can keep appealing to their anxiety and fundamental addiction to significance through the success and certainty that you promise to provide them with.

In the light of such titillating flattery most of us tend to miss the deafening realities threaded through our complex and blood soaked story:

Adolf Hitler was amongst the most successful motivational speakers of all time.

Jimmy Saville was amongst the most successful presenters and philanthropists of his generation.

The Daily Telegraph reports that a recent study of 261 Senior Business Executives in the USA suggested that at least 1 in 5 displayed many traits of fully fledged psychopathy.

More recently, the most successful military coalition in human history, retaliating to an attack by 19 men that killed 2,996 people, invaded developing countries in the Middle East resulting in the deaths of a figure already in the hundreds of thousands and steadily growing – many of them civilians and children. Simultaneously, domestic gun laws mean that according to the US Centre for Disease Control & Prevention, more than 30,000 of the US civilians soldiers are giving their precious lives to protect, are slain by one another each year.

None of it makes any sense.

You see, our level of accumulated power, success, fame and influence is no more an indicator of true wisdom and value in our lives than is our height or hair colour.

But this is too painful a reality for us to face.

What a peculiar irony for our race that those lives that have exponentially impacted us most for eternal good, invariably ended in failure and tragedy:

Martin Luther King; persecuted, incarcerated and executed.

Gandhi, persecuted, incarcerated and executed.

Jesus, persecuted, incarcerated, and executed.

Nelson Mandela, persecuted and incarcerated –

Revolutionary lives amongst countless others who have shared the same fate at the hands of their fellow 'civilised' man in societies desperate to silence their voices.

Even so and what remains; echoing throughout our disfigured history; is that still small voice that reminds us that a *true Leader will surely speak to us in mystery and complexity leaving us with questions* rather than the self-assured snake-oil patter promising to make us rich and solve all of our issues, should we follow and worship our contemporary halfwit-Tsars of certainty.

May we wonder on these things and quietly and patiently think.

May we increasingly reflect upon how we might use the remarkable and revolutionary resources that modern technology now affords us to encourage our fragile race to understand and believe in its own intrinsic value *apart* from success.

Imagine a generation who were encouraged and nurtured to prioritise their self-awareness, their relationships, their creativity, and the fruitfulness available to them that they might nurture and develop in a world quite literally gasping for air as it becomes strangled by the accelerating desire of human hunger.

If we scale chronological history down to one year – with the Big Bang on January 1st – our species, *homo sapiens* does not even appear until 11:59 on December 31st.

Our modern civilisation and culture only exist in the final nanosecond of that day.

You see, the earth does not belong to us.

We belong to it.

The truth does not belong to us.

We belong to it.

God does not belong to us.

We belong to Her.

Instead of using the magnificent knowledge and opportunities at our disposal for truth and for good, it is possible that in parts of the world, we are becoming blinder and more lost than we may understand until it is too late.

There is an ancient story in which a student gently asked his wise teacher;

'In the olden days there were many who saw the face of God. Why don't they now?'

And the Teacher replied;

'Because nowadays, no-one can stoop so low.'

Reflect:

What has represented true success in *your* life?

What have you sacrificed to pursue this?

Do the outcomes of this seem good or bad?

Might you prioritise differently in the future?

Wealth is Measured in Relationships

One of the experiences that has most influenced my work happened several years ago when I was invited by a friend to Alcoholics Anonymous.

It is an organisation that he has been involved in as a member and as a sponsor in several countries, and though I had always wanted to go, I had never had the courage or opportunity.

I was intrigued, because I have spent my working life trying to build and develop therapeutic communities to provide people with a safe context in which to face issues, change and grow. Consequently, I have studied a lot about AA and remember being moved by a particularly compelling description of a meeting by one of my favourite writers in which he was affected deeply by the mutual dependence of the members.

As the group convened, the confidentiality rules and format were explained to me and my friend told his fascinating story of childhood hurt and alienation, his steady descent into anxiety, drugs and then prison, violence, alcoholism and then gradually, the beginnings of recovery and a slow and purposed walk of healing and change via the 12 steps.

As he finished and the group thanked him, others began to quietly contribute from their own lives and experiences. As different people spoke in that little backroom I was struck by both the unity of diverse people and the feeling of complete safety conveyed by the group, making it possible for one another to share with honesty and openness.

Individuals of all ages, from several countries, at all stages and every possible walk of life talked nakedly, freely, humbly; about their own struggles, daily need for change and their sincere hope for healing and Redemption.

For the next hour, I hunched increasingly lower in my plastic chair biting my knuckle so that I wouldn't cry, as story after story after story acknowledged the teller's brokenness and then desire for real change and complete dependence on the little community for daily progress and survival. I found to my surprise that the increasingly overwhelming emotion that I was feeling was longing, coupled with the frustration and sadness that the profoundly freeing principles I was seeing so simply displayed were distinctly lacking in many of the therapeutic and supportive contexts I had been involved in.

More than ever they seem overwhelmingly absent in our so-called 'connected' society. I fear that that they may lack even more in our families and in our closest relationships.

Over the course of the next few days I thought endlessly about what I had witnessed. I felt somehow that I couldn't let this experience go, that I had to do something.

As I thought and agonised, I realised that ultimately, the only way to respond to what I had seen was to somehow try to start a community myself that might replicate the safety and reality of AA. I wondered if it might be possible to find a way to learn and to follow the 12 steps of recovery; whatever an individual's circumstances, in a context of complete openness, honesty and mutual dependence.

I hoped that a group might form and experiment with a traditional AA format: 30 minutes of catch up, a 30 minute talk by one member and then 30 minutes of discussion. As I began to contact friends to describe the idea, I found to my amazement and relief that the response was immediate and overwhelming and nearly everyone I tentatively approached wanted to do all they could to be involved.

A week later, a little core of 4 of us met and considered the right venue and a few evenings later we gathered, nervous, not really knowing what we had let ourselves in for as we sat around drinking coffee.

The group was made up of a real diversity; ten or so individuals from a great range of backgrounds, all walks of life with differing affiliations, family situations, experiences and yet the shared desire and hope and commitment for openness, community and a shared pursuit of progress.

We discussed four principles that we felt should be central to what we were doing; foundations that I think must apply to any attempt at building a safe context of reflection and community:

Confidentiality: all that was shared in the group would stay in the group and not be shared outside of it.

Acceptance: we were here to establish a context in which one another's thoughts, struggles, dilemmas and person-alities could and would be accepted and valued regardless of our understanding and agreement. We would seek to maintain unity and encourage and nurture one another at all costs.

Non-disclosure: Though we wanted a context in which people felt they could pour out their hearts and share their deepest struggles, such disclosure was not a requirement for membership and it was fine just to be there and to lis-ten; no-one would be pressured or expected to share unless they felt completely comfortable to do so.

Support: we aimed and hoped to be able to support one another and establish a shared interdependence; if some-one expressed a need, concern or hurt with which they were struggling, then the group and the other individuals would hope and desire to support that person without set-ting conditions or demands.

Without going into detail I can simply say that to all of our surprise, the floodgates were blown open that first night. I had wondered if openness and trust might take several months, but almost immediately and without any hint of invitation, intensely moving and personal stories of suffer-ing, struggles, progress, hope and victory were shared and listened to, tears were shed between us and the birth of a little community took place.

We went far beyond the allotted time and finally I remember that someone spoke up and said in a voice thick with emotion that he had travelled the world and waited 28 years for a group such as this. We sat quietly for a few moments, and then hugged and left, surprised and hopeful about what might be to come.

Many years on, I look back on the incredible journey that started that night between us as we met weekly for several years thereafter; intertwining our lives with a regularity and commitment that deeply affected us all.

A small number of peripheral members came and went, but the core of us remained steadfast on a committed journey of mutual inter-dependence.

We argued, laughed and wept together. We supported one another through that which life will most certainly bring: the births of children, bereavement, illness, relationship struggles and career and parenting challenges of every kind.

We made some naive mistakes.

Sometimes things were an enormous struggle and we should have been more aware of so much that we later learnt and are still learning about the nature of community.

Tragically, one of our founding members who had been suffering from severe depression and anxiety took his own life and we struggled with guilt and mourned his death, carrying one another through the great loss.

We also celebrated many joys and triumphs as we struggled forward as a group. We were privileged to see incredible growth and healing in so many of our situations and families.

More than anything, we grew and changed and learnt to share our failures and our successes as a community, rather than living simply as individuals.

We learnt to face life with one another; and to overcome together.

Finally, after several years, people moved away, got married, different jobs; circumstances changed and the 30/30/30 community naturally drew to an end. Although 3 of us still meet regularly, our lives in the wider group eventually grew outwards and that particular 'season' has now passed.

But the shared story of our group has had a considerable effect on me and informed all of the work that I have done since.

I continue to work therapeutically with a wide range of people whether in a Business Context directing awareness and development, or in the homeless projects that I oversee for vulnerable young teenagers.

I have experienced so very many days in which I might support a 16-year-old struggling with the anxieties and challenges of caring for her new born baby in the morning, and then in the afternoon discuss the stresses of sales with a Business Director.

And more and more, I see that in our diverse human family, regardless of our material situation, our most fundamental psychological needs are invariably: just the same.

Whoever we are, as people, parents and leaders we face the most complex and overwhelming array of conflicting priorities, anxieties, stresses and challenges to balance and overcome in the relentless pressure of our modern lives.

Whatever our circumstances, what we seem to lack most is a safe place in which we can think upon, consider and maybe share the deep questions – that which we are really feeling and struggling with.

Perhaps more than anything else in our busy and complicated lives, we need somewhere in which we can rest and think; where we know that we will simply be listened to and treated with gentleness and respect.

Through experiences of inspiring success and also of painful failure, I have spent my working life trying to provide such a refuge for people, whether it be with a group of business leaders directing reflective practice, or in a safe house for those from abusive backgrounds.

I still believe that no other place will give us the opportunity to do that which is most crucial;

...to think, reflect and then to invest in ourselves.

Nothing else brings progress or change.

Reflect:

Would you like to belong to a Life group like this?

Are there people you know who might want to join?

How could you begin the process of building such a group?

When will you start?

In Conclusion

Thank you for joining me in this season of your journey.

I hope, with all of my heart, that the thoughts and themes that we have considered and reflected upon will prove to be an inspiration and a blessing to you in your precious life and relationships – just as they have proved so to me over these many years.

I want to close by returning finally to the four principles introduced at the start of this book and leave them with you; in the hope that they may become foundational in the same way that they have been and continue to be such a precious bedrock to me.

I hope that they will remain in your heart.

I know that if they do, they will surely protect you and keep you rooted in goodness and grace.

Thank you for walking with me in this season.

Love and peace to you as you walk onwards on your journey.

I hope that we will meet one day.

What You Are Looking For is not Out There.
It is Within You.
Helen Keller

Awareness

The foundational understanding of our lives should be that in every moment, every hour and in every day that we draw breath, we are here to *learn*. At all costs must we stay open, curious and committed to pursuing those things which we have not realised or understood yet. If we become wise, we will find that the number of them increases, rather than decreases, as we grow older.

We must learn to welcome uncertainty and mystery rather than the simplistic answers, categories and external distractions that are constantly forced upon us. Instead, we would do well to make our inner journey the primary pursuit of our lives. We will have to work tirelessly over many years to discover who we are within – but only in finding and knowing ourself will we ever know true freedom.

This is because, despite what culture will try to sell us, everything that we need for the journey is already within us, like treasure waiting to be found.

Only in first digging for and then disciplining and harnessing our true nature, will we ever have anything of any worth to offer or contribute.

Before we can love or give to anybody, we must first learn to know and then to become completely comfortable with who we are.

The greatest enemy we must ever conquer, and the greatest battles that we will ever fight; are within us. It will surely hurt when it is revealed how weak we can be, how broken by life, and how selfish. But we must accept this pain and never flee from the reality of our paradoxical true humanity.

Instead, we must balance our needs and weaknesses with the staggering beauty and the glory that is so precious within us.

We will not have to search for this glory, it will simply make itself known to us as we bravely explore, and the more humble and curious we allow ourselves to be, the more we will recognise its presence.

We only need learn to live in the balance of the dark and the light that make up who we really are, with no attempt to suppress either.

Then we will be able to choose good with our whole heart.

We must ultimately understand that there is nothing of any worth in all of human life that can be gained without us taking responsibility for and mastering our own will.

Our bravery in taking this responsibility on a daily basis is the most powerful thing that will ever be available to us.

If we protect it at all costs it will serve us well.

Change

The only thing that will be certain in life until we die, is that things and people around us will change. If we possibly can, we must try to accept this inevitability, rather than to fight it.

Change is frightening and we tend to naturally fear it and do our best to avoid it, but the energy we will expend fighting, is completely wasted.

Better to use such energy to learn how to surf the changes that come, and to try to enjoy riding the waves. Occasionally we will fall, and find ourselves hurt, maybe even damaged by the storms.

But only the falling will strengthen and equip us for the larger waves to come.

If we fail to accept and learn the rhythmic dance of fall and rise, we will never be capable of enjoying the greatest opportunities, the most thrilling rides.

The most crucial ability we can ever develop is the willingness to humbly stop and to change because we are learning. Only then can we become strong enough to apologise when we are wrong, and when we hurt other people.

And as we grow older, we must learn to change more, rather than less.

Stagnation and pride are the most dangerous enemies of all, because they will come to us dressed as success, wealth and position.

We must only ever accept such symbols if we are at a place where we know we can master them and use them for our growth. Otherwise, they will slowly drown us and we will not be aware of it.

Relationships

Wealth is measured in relationships.

We must prioritise people, and seek to learn as much as we possibly can from others at every stage of our journey. If we are wise, we will learn from each and every single person we ever meet. We must never discard other people's opinions or perspectives because they threaten or scare us. Instead we must think long and hard about everything that we see and hear.

Then we can learn to prioritise and follow those people that are real, and in whom we find integrity and joy.

We are wisest to seek friends, fellow travellers and trusted colleagues of all ages, and when we have found them, be willing to lay down our life for them.

We will know who our true friends are, because they will be the people that in being our true self, we find ourselves completely safe with. As we share what is on our heart with them we must always invite them to tell us what they really think, as we explore our struggles and adventures.

We must listen quietly to the things they share, remembering that a true friend will 'stab us in the front'.

For without loving accountability, we will learn nothing and be nobody in this life. If only we are brave and wise enough to pursue real relationships like this, we will find true wealth.

Many people will tell us to 'follow our heart' with the best intentions – but this is an illusion. Instead, we need first submit to the work that results in us knowing our heart. Then the path ahead will become absolutely clear.

If we possibly can, we might delay the big decisions in life for as long as we feel possible. Few of us seem to marry wisely; not because we lack love, but because we lack patience.

May we celebrate aloneness for as long as we possibly can.

Fruitfulness

Most importantly of all things; we must not waste this precious life pursuing security, wealth or success.

Instead, we must make the absolute goal of our lives to become fruitful; like a tree, planted deep by a river, that as it grows, provides shade and sustenance for those around it.

If we can grow into such a tree through these years, we will find that it will be the greatest glory of our life.

We must seek in all ways, and at all times, to live in a way that honours and nourishes the values that will become sacred to us; our deep passion, our aching soul; and in this way we will find that we will impact those around us, for good.

This is not complicated or hard – if only we bravely persist in pursuing awareness, change and relationships and then be willing to grow in the light of our ongoing discovery.

It is only this journey that will lead towards the unlocking of our true purpose.

Then we will know what it is that we must do with our life, and in doing it with our whole heart, we will spread our branches, and bear fruit in others.

As we grow old, we will realise that this fruit is the only thing we will leave behind us of any value.

Finally, we might think on this.

The adventure and wonder and pain of this great journey will sometimes be too much to bear.

In these times, we must remember that life is meant to be difficult.

In every moment that we can accept this challenge and let the ever changing weather of life gently bear fruit in us, the rain of night will become a friend to us and the warmth of the sunrise, closer.

For:

The planet does not need more 'successful' people.

The planet desperately needs more peacemakers, healers, restorers, storytellers and lovers of every kind.

– The Dalai Llama

About the author

John Richards was born in Exeter in the UK in 1976, later moving to North Portugal where he studied for an International Baccalaureate at the multi-national OBS; the oldest British School in Europe. John read English Literature at Queen Mary and Westfield College, the University of London, from where he graduated in 1996.

In his early twenties, John started his career in Crisis Intervention, working with a vast range of vulnerable people including both the victims and perpetrators of severe abuse, street homeless teenagers, asylum seekers, and numerous other complex client groups in need of safety and change.

John's specialism became the leadership and development of 24hr staffed therapeutic communities focused on the healing and growth of vulnerable young people. He has specialised in this area for over 18 years as a practitioner and then operational leader for a national provider.

More recently, John founded AwarenessChange.Com, a consultancy for Businesses, Organisations and Individuals focused around a range of transformative personal development offers including Awareness Retreats and Intensive 1:1 work.

Currently, he works in partnership with Neil Laughton, the multi-award winning Explorer and Business Coach, and Angus Wingfield, the Director and founder of Africa Wild Trails, to lead The Inspiration Programme.

TIP is a development programme in the UK, Africa and the Himalayas, providing individuals and businesses with opportunity for adventure, conservation and personal inspiration in order to achieve their greatest potential.

John is a widely read writer who has been published by Action for Happiness and The Goodall Foundation.

If you would like to attend an Awareness Retreat to work on your life story, join us on The Inspiration Programme in the UK, Africa or the Himalayas, or work 1:1 with John, please contact:

john@awarenesschange.com

Background:

I wrote part one of this book several years ago when I found myself suddenly poorly and bed-bound. A few weeks before, I had spent a night on the acute care ward after having collapsed with severe exhaustion and chest pains, and was subsequently told by the Consultant that I had a suspected double Pulmonary embolism and might not survive the night. It was a tremendous shock – I was 36.

It made me think a lot about what I really believe in; and those things that I have found myself thinking so much about over these many years.

The morning after – to my tremendous relief – it was discovered that I was actually suffering from a form of severe viral pleurisy, but I was told that I couldn't return to my busy schedule for several months.

With time finally on my hands, I found myself sitting up through the painful nights of shallow laborious breathing, and writing about my accumulated thoughts as I slowly recovered and my chest healed.

I have added the chapters and themes in Part 2 over the years since.

As I wrote during that first month, I thought a lot about what I wanted to do if I ever got better, and what really mattered to me. I was full of anxiety and beset by the night terrors I have suffered all my life. I wondered if I would

ever make a full recovery and be able to breathe and walk
properly again.

One sleepless and anxious night, I wrote these lines, which
seem to describe my hopes and fears better than I am able
now:

Covered in familiar shards of twisted thought,
that pierce the skin. But not too deep
to warrant bathes and salve.
From far within
I search to find
a safety valve
that might slow and ebb this constant tide
of slow distort.

Hour upon hour, life upon life.
shadow enemies dice and devour
my peace with silent knife.

This well worn path;
I see my boyhood footprints
small and soft, beside me now.
And wonder that I am returning here
as if he were calling:
and I so familiar to this way of fear
feel again I am falling,
falling.

I have so much, I am so much. I am not a victim.
Kindness surrounds me like a moat.

But in these desperate hours, I am far, so far from all hope
and utterly remote.

Still, though these constant dreads allay me
strangling my fevered mind above,
yet I long that far below me,
I may leave a trail of love.

Acknowledgements

Without the following people, this book would not have been possible:

George Stoimenov, The Sash, Nathaniel Robin, Billy, Chandra, Nick Morley, The Burns, Andy Venner, James Andrews, Peter Rabbit, Jon Badders, Ash, Mike & Viv, Merv & Dee, Nikki Lascelles, Les Wheeldon, Vickie Blair, Mrs M, Mark Williamson, Penny Diver, Ann-Marie Marshall, Emma Horne, Louisa Watkin, Mark, Denise and all at RoL, Everyone at Phoenix and HG, Simon Gale, Ollie Aplin, Tsering and Nima – All key companions on the journey.

Diane Allen, for her ongoing encouragement, wisdom and patient editing.

Mark Middlemiss and JD.

Neil Laughton and Angus Wingfield.

Todd; for your unfailing faith in this book.

John Venner; a second Dad to me for so many years – I miss you.

Keith Robertson – a 'friend who sticks closer than a brother'.

Finally, to my Family: Dad, Mum, Anna, Ess, Maddie, Bells, Rosie, the Ev, the twins and AJ.

... and most of all, E&H.

Thank you.

JR – September 2018

EYEWEAR PUBLISHING

Eyewear publishes fiction,
non-fiction, and poetry.

Recent prose works include:
Barbell Buddha by Chris Moore
Positiverosity by David Fox-Pitt
The Virtuous Cyborg by Chris Bateman
Eagles and Earwigs by Colin Wilson
That Summer in Puglia by Valeria Vescina
Juggling With Turnips by Karl MacDermott
Aliens, Gods & Artists by Sam Eisenstein
Last Performance At The Odeon by Carol Susan Nathanson
The Other Side Of Como by Mara G. Fox

WWW.EYEWEARPUBLISHING.COM